Arbitral Travels

Arbitral Travels

Reminiscences of a Peripatetic Jamaican Arbitrator

M.J. STOPPI

The University of the West Indies Press

Jamaica • Barbados • Trinidad and Tobago

The University of the West Indies Press
7A Gibraltar Hall Road, Mona
Kingston 7, Jamaica
www.uwipress.com

A catalogue record of this book is available from
the National Library of Jamaica.

ISBN: 978-976-640-693-6 (print)
978-976-640-694-3 (Kindle)
978-976-640-695-0 (ePub)

Cover and book design by Robert Harris
Set in Minion Pro 11/15 x 24

Printed in the United States of America.

In loving memory of my parents,

Nathan and Fanny Stoppi

Contents

Foreword

International arbitration is the preferred dispute resolution process for cross-border disputes, because arbitration awards are enforceable under the New York Convention in more than 148 countries around the world. Judgements of local domestic courts are not as readily enforceable, and in many jurisdictions, the judgement of a court from another jurisdiction cannot be enforced without a "re-run" of the trial.

The Government of Jamaica is committed to sustainable economic development, recognizing that investors need assurance that they are conducting business in an economically stable environment. The legal risks inherent in transactional business ventures (particularly cross-border commercial arrangements) demand a settlement dispute mechanism that is expedient, cognizant of emerging trends, and that operates at a modernized level.

With the enactment of the Arbitration Act, 2017, Jamaica has joined more than seventy countries worldwide and more than one hundred jurisdictions. This act has brought the United Nations Commission on International Trade Law (UNCITRAL) Model Law into domestic legislation; and when complemented by the Convention on the Recognition and Enforcement of Foreign Arbitral Awards (also known as the New York Convention), which Jamaica ratified on 10 July 2002, the strong signal is sent that we are serious about creating the right environment for investment.

The Mona International Centre for Arbitration and Mediation is in full operation. The centre's visionary move ensured that once the legislative framework was established, there was already a modernized venue to host arbitration disputes and provide the requisite training. As a result, Jamaica has a credible and well-trained cadre of arbitrators who will join the existing illustrious panel of arbitrators worldwide.

The launch of *Arbitral Travels* by Maurice Stoppi, one of the most highly respected and internationally recognized arbitration experts, is indeed another positive message to the international community. What makes it particularly significant is that he is a Jamaican, and the book is being launched in Jamaica.

We need nothing else to prove to the world that we are ready.

Congratulations, Maurice.

Delroy Chuck, QC, MP
Minister of Justice, Government of Jamaica
June 2018

Preface

An arbitrator – for those innocent, and perhaps young and fortunate enough, never to have had the pleasure and privilege of meeting one face-to-face – is a rare breed: part lawyer, part technician, part masochist, and part (no one has yet discovered which part) human being. Arbitrators come in various flavours: some salty, some sour, and some – very rarely – rather sweet. In their native habitat, they may also be observed in a variety of genders, heights, degrees of corpulence, but all share one characteristic: a marked absence of any discernible sense of humour.

Most – certainly among those with whom I have had the dubious pleasure of coming into contact – reach the status of arbitrator after mastering the vicissitudes of some other profession or vocation, typically law, or possibly one of the nobler professions such as quantity surveying, architecture or engineering.

I mention quantity surveying because that is where I started. I did not wake up one morning long ago and say to myself, "All my role models of today – such as Errol Flynn, Aristotle Onassis or Yuri Gagarin – have one thing in common, and that is the path I wish to forge for myself on this planet." Far from it. I woke up that morning very hungry and decided that everything I had been told was indeed true. If I wanted to eat, I had to go and find a job! I was a young, thin lad in those days; and neither wishing, nor able, to get any thinner, I took a flying leap into the first Situations Vacant position that would accept me: that of office boy in a quantity surveyor's office.

Since this is a story about arbitrators, the thrills and spills of my rise to professional fame (alas, but not fortune) in the roller-coaster world of quantity surveying must be reserved for another occasion. Suffice it to say that there comes a time in the life of many a professional when a greater, though not necessarily more lucrative, calling presents itself as an extension to one's core activity – be it by design, by accident, or as a natural progression of one's existing vocation.

So it was in my case. At the time, the key to the dizzying heights of the quantity surveying profession was to pass the final examination of the Royal Institution of Chartered Surveyors. My route was the tortuous but ultimately successful preparation for the dreaded final exam, which notably included several introductory courses into legal matters such as property law, tort law, common law and arbitration law. These "baby steps" into the law appealed to me on several counts – not the least of which was their call for clear exposition, logic, debate and an ability to discern truth from argument.

My entry, then, into the mysteries of the law was by the back door. I did not see this originally as a handicap, since it enabled me to serve initially as a reasonably knowledgeable construction professional, expert witness or adviser to those arguing cases before qualified arbitrators. The rest is history: admittance to the Institute of Arbitrators (as it was then known) on Cannon Street, London, followed by fellowship of both the Royal Institution of Chartered Surveyors and the Chartered Institute of Arbitrators (as it later became known), and, since the 1970s, acting as a sole arbitrator.

The basic principles of arbitration – from biblical times to the present – have remained essentially unchanged: that of disputants calling upon the intervention and decision of an independent third party to settle their differences. The practice of arbitration, however, has, over time, evolved dramatically. Rapidly vanishing are the days of the individual technical arbitrator hearing evidence in layman's terms and delivering well-reasoned technical decisions in equally familiar language to all concerned. Today, with the rapid growth in commerce and international contracts, arbitrations have become vastly more complex and firmly founded on legal principles. The beard-stroking, pipe-smoking archetype of a friendly umpire has given way to individual or entire teams of high-powered multilingual lawyers backed by electronic support systems and institutional arrangements.

Having started, as I did, in the beard-stroking days and having made the transition to the electronic era, I have penned here some notes of my arbitral experiences in the hope that they may be of interest to practitioners of the art, as well as students preparing to make the leap into the deep end of arbitral practice. Readers should be aware that all Jamaican cases mentioned in this book took place prior to the enactment of The Arbitration Act, 2017; therefore the applicable statute law then operative was Jamaica's Arbitration Act of 1900.

Finally, I wish to offer my thanks to Dr Christopher Malcolm, attorney-at-law and senior lecturer in the Faculty of Law, University of the West Indies, Mona, and secretary-general of the Jamaica International Arbitration Centre, for his invaluable assistance in the preparation of this book, as well as to my son Jonathan Stoppi for his help in mastering the vagaries of English grammar.

M.J. Stoppi
Kingston, Jamaica
July 2017

Part 1.

Cases

1.

Arbitral Baptism

Let us rewind now, back to the early 1960s, where we find a young, thin – albeit no longer skeletal – but already well-experienced quantity surveyor setting up a tiny, penniless embryonic Jamaican practice in the heady, opulent, pre-independence atmosphere of Montego Bay. My brief professional career until then, fraught with contradictions, driven more by events than by design or prudent planning, had led me here in a bid to escape the colonial stranglehold on my chosen profession in Kingston (which is another story).

I shared an office on Union Street with an American architect, with whom I had worked before as a quantity surveyor on small house additions or school extensions. In addition, I had managed to acquire one or two clients of my own.

The object of this particular tale was a house – no ordinary house, mind you, but a vacation villa complex for a wealthy American industrialist, soon to retire, on a site adjoining the Flint River: a spectacular, lush river that wound its way lazily from the heights of the Cockpit Country of western Jamaica, down to the sea, past the village of Hopewell next to the famous Round Hill Hotel. The site itself was idyllic: fairly flat, overlooking the bamboo-lined banks of the river to the west and the tropical forest to the east, with a magnificent view of the St James parish coastline, a reef-protected deep-green bay and the azure-blue beyond. The contract sum for the project, including all external works, was in the region of 44,000 Jamaican pounds – an enormous amount even by the standards of that time.

The architect, who happened to be the client's son-in-law, was a bit of an oddball– tall, lanky and Hungarian, with an overly anglicized name, almost a caricature of himself. His working drawings for his father-in-law's proposed residence were abysmal, making it difficult for me to produce

3

the bid documents and bills of quantities. His wife, also an architect, was, from the little I saw of her on their occasional visits to their local associate architect, dressed in the height of *Vogue* tropical fashion. She served as both associate architect and owner's daughter; the phase "conflict of interest" came easily to mind.

To make matters even more interesting, the architects decided to delegate the job of supervision of the construction to yet another colourful Montego Bay character – equally flamboyant and also Eastern European – with a name comprising more consonants than vowels. Unlike the architect, he was only – if I remember correctly – about five-and-a-bit feet tall, and he compensated his lack of height by chain-smoking through a long, slim holder that he used as much for affectation as for emphasis, while chattering away in pidgin English. This habit proved challenging on-site and amusing to onlookers, particularly when he attempted to give instructions to his Jamaican contractors. They understood little of what he was asking of them, and he, equally, did not understand most of their Jamaican Patois replies, which were not always complimentary.

The contractors were the well-established north-coast firm of Maffessanti and Filisetti. Prior to the Second World War, I was told, Messrs M. and F. were itinerant Italian terrazzo and marble craftsmen, and they, like many of their compatriots, had been plying their trade in Allied territories as war commenced in 1939. The father of Maffessanti, having been discovered by the British colonial authorities in Ghana, was interned by the colonial British government in Jamaica for the duration of the war. Internment was at Gibraltar Camp (see practice note 1) – a collection of wooden barracks in a prolific mango orchard in the Mona estate of suburban Kingston (now the home of the University of the West Indies). Bizarrely, the same camp was used to house many European refugees from Nazism, whom the British authorities, not knowing quite what to do with them on their arrival, simply bundled together with the enemy aliens. Before long, however, the two disparate groups began to mingle and eventually established a functioning and violent-free polyglot community. Once the war was over, Maffessanti and Filisetti, having developed a liking for the local food (and possibly also the local by-products of distilled sugar cane), opted to stay in Jamaica rather than return to their native habitats. They then sent for their family members, formed a nascent terrazzo company in Jamaica, and subsequently applied their construction skills on the island.

Returning to the point of this story, after the project began, I attended project site meetings – in part because as the project quantity surveyor, it was my professional obligation to do so, but also so as not to miss out on the entertaining experience of the Montego Bay equivalent of the Tower of Babel. I often recalled the then popular British radio comedy programme *The Goon Show;* any one of the site meetings would have qualified as a segment.

As the contract proceeded, the architects were rarely seen on-site. When decisions, usually change orders and variations, were to be given, they were merely communicated to the short, cigarette-smoking supervisor in Montego Bay. Struggling to understand the contract or the bills of quantities, the supervisor would complain about construction details, and when told that they were in accordance with local practice, he responded with a series of unintelligible comments amid a foul-smelling miasma of cigarette smoke. The situation was made even worse when, on their rare visits to the site, the architects countermanded the supervisor's instructions and issued other, conflicting changes. The result caused both difficulties and delays on the site, but also much amusement to local onlookers, who, though still mystified by the supervisor's speech, fully understood the workmen's patois responses. Various items, occasionally vital to the project, were left out of the design, and with the innumerable changes made in the course of construction, the final contract value total bore little relationship to that which I had stated in the bill of quantities.

Eventually the house was completed, and it indeed looked pleasing. Well proportioned, it met the approval of the client's representatives and all who visited. There was one small problem, however. The client's daughter proved unwilling to present the true cost of the contract to Papa, who no doubt would have held her and her architect husband responsible for the gross cost overruns. The result was predictable: valuation certificates presented and not paid, all manner of excuses from the client's representative and architect (no suggestion of a conflict of interest yet!), demands for payment by contractors and so on. Threats to quit the project were pointless, since it had been completed by the contractors in good faith. A full-fledged dispute was born – to be settled, as required by their contract requirements, by arbitration.

Since the building contract used was the then standard American Institute of Architects form, the parties could choose between a sole arbitrator or a panel. And although the scope and importance of the dispute did not warrant a panel arbitration, the clients opted for one: one arbitrator appointed by each party, and a third, an umpire, nominated by the two appointees. The claimant (the contractors) chose D.G.M. Chalmers, an architect from Kingston, as their nominee; the respondent chose architect T.T. Crenshaw of Puerto Rico. These two appointed the then *custos rotolariam* (see practice note 4) of the parish of Hanover, the Honourable W.H. deLisser, as their referee, or umpire. For legal counsel, the claimant chose a distinguished local barrister, Mr Daniel Lett, instructed by Messrs Robinson Phillips and Whitehorne of Ocho Rios; the respondent selected Mr Richard Mahfood, instructed by Messrs Milholland, Ashenheim and Stone, attorneys-at-law of Kingston. With this imposing cast of characters, totally disproportionate to the issue, proceedings got underway.

How did I come into all this rather heady stuff as a young, newly qualified quantity surveyor? Simply by virtue of recently passing the external final exams of the then Institute of Arbitrators, which designated me as a fully fledged member. This being something of a rarity in Jamaica, and it becoming known that I had a passing knowledge of English law and arbitral procedure, I received an invitation to join the team of the claimant as a technical adviser from Lieutenant Colonel (Retired) Hurlstone St Clair "Hurley" Whitehorne of the contractors' firm of solicitors Robinson, Phillips and Whitehorne. After the usual interlocutory procedures, the hearing venue was selected by the umpire, who, as president at the time of the Hanover Polo Club, chose to hold the hearings at his club (taking particular care to position his chair for a view of the polo field and the magnificent coastline and Caribbean Sea beyond). Proceedings were set to begin on 20 May 1963.

Meanwhile, I continued to earn my daily crust as a lowly quantity surveyor in a corner of the architect's office. One morning, before the hearings began but after I had prepared the presentation of the contractors' claims, the secretary knocked on my door to announce the unscheduled visit of the architect's wife.

What on earth can she possibly want with me? I thought. Had I said the wrong thing at one of our meetings? I was still mentally speculating, when she entered and, smilingly sweetly and extending a limp, cool hand for me to grasp, slid into a chair adjoining my desk and half whispered, "Good morning, Mr Stoppi."

To say that I was caught unawares would be an understatement. I remember mumbling a response, which must have sounded rather incoherent to her. She began telling me how much she was impressed, not only by me but by the British system of quantity surveying as a whole – a profession then unknown in her country – but, above all, how she admired me as a man, as a technician and so on.

I was overwhelmed. Here she was, having taken the trouble to come to see me – me of all people – dressed in her Sunday best complete with matching accessories: fashionable straw hat, and small, square straw handbag, which she had placed at the edge of the desk. I was, to be honest, both flattered and more than a little confused. Had she really just come to see me because she liked me? Did I make that much of an impression? My musings were interrupted by her request that we meet later that evening for drinks at the yacht club.

Well! That was it – goodbye discretion, hello adventure! I was now ego-driven, so much so that I could hardly keep up my end of what I mistakenly took for a flirtation. I mumbled something about how honoured I was, and yes, I'd love to, and so on. Apparently, however, I was not as coherent as she would have wished, for she asked me to repeat my response, while casually sliding her straw handbag across the desk towards me.

That's when I woke up. When I asked what was in her purse, her demeanour instantly changed. "What do you mean? How dare you!" she stormed.

Without answering, I grabbed her straw box, opened the lid, and, as I had suspected, found inside a small tape recorder, in motion. Without a word, I removed the tape and placed it in my desk drawer. I experienced a cascade of emotions: the initial gratification by the false flattery was replaced by indignation that anyone would stoop to such scheming, followed quickly by pride that she considered my testimony against her side of the dispute to be of such value that I should be worth compromising.

At this point, she was speechless. Always the gentleman, I told her that if

I reported this matter to the arbitrators, her father's case would be irreparably damaged, but that out of recognition of her loyalty and immature desire to help her father's case, I would avoid doing so. However, I added sternly that if there were a repetition of this or any similar act, I would have no hesitation reporting her. Within seconds, she regained her composure, sweetly thanked me for the interview and said she looked forward to seeing me again at the hearing.

The hearings began on schedule, and when presenting my evidence, I was ably led by our attorney in presenting my evidence, which by logic and priced quantities supported the value of the contractor's claim, with regard both to the details of traditional forms of Jamaican construction and to the calculation of local building costs. There was little the defence could present to counter our claims, which in the view of our legal team were both contractually correct and properly costed. The hearings continued with each of the technical arbitrators posing their own questions, as needed. The umpire played little part in the proceedings, apart from acceding to occasional requests from the arbitrators to snore not quite so loudly, or, when awake, issuing sudden and peremptory instructions to the club steward to fetch him his favourite drink! Under the efficient and guiding hand of the two technical arbitrators, the hearings continued uneventfully for another two or three days, until they felt they had concluded their assignment. Two months later, on 29 July 1963, they published a unanimous award in favour of the claimants, our clients.

This, then, was my first taste of a formal construction arbitration in Jamaica. Apart from the professional satisfaction of being on the winning side, it gave me an appreciation of the importance of proper contract documentation, keeping current records in writing, and conforming to contract conditions. It also gave me an insight into the legal side of construction disputes – an interest that has not waned in the forty or more years since then – and the added benefit of a lifelong friendship and professional relationship with the lawyers and contractors with whom I worked on our side of the action. Last but not least, it opened my wondering eyes – like a drama student attending his first professional Shakespearean production – to the mind-expanding world of law, logic and equity.

2.

Taking the Oath

Prior to the development of indigenous arbitral legislation, most of the current legislation in the Caribbean region was simply a clone of the English act of 1950, which in turn was based on the English act of 1900, which has long been recognized by progressive lawmakers in the United Kingdom as archaic and hopelessly out of date. In a bid to modernize the entire approach to arbitral procedure, a new English act was passed in 1979 that was somewhat more appropriate to the contemporary British justice system and commercial realities.

Towards the end of the twentieth century, competition in the burgeoning business of arbitration – especially in the settlement of international disputes – began to emerge in Hong Kong, New York and other regional centres. This was mainly due to both their modern and relevant legislation governing the practice of aribitration, which was required for the efficient processing of international commercial disputes. In a bid to retain its premier position in international arbitration, British lawmakers radically revised the English act yet again, resulting in the new act of 1996. Meanwhile, we poor ex-colonials, still umbilically connected to the original 1889 act, patiently awaited the promulgation of our own arbitral legislation as befitting both our relationship to Westminster and Caribbean culture. Several Caribbean states have produced their own updated law (some based upon that of the United Nations Commission on International Trade Law [UNCITRAL]). Jamaica only recently followed, resulting in the new Arbitration Act, 2017, also based on the UNCITRAL Model Law (see practice note 9). However, all Jamaican cases cited in this volume predate 2017 and refer to the original English 1900 law.

By way of illustration, let me tell you about Mr Conrad Rutkovsky. Prior to the 1970s, he was the civil engineer partner of the firm of Rutkovsky and Bradford, a Kingston firm with whom my firm of quantity surveyors did much consulting work. Both he and his architect partner were also social acquaintances of mine. Fast forward now to the early 1990s, where I am sitting as sole arbitrator in a construction arbitration in Grand Cayman (although measuring only twenty-one by seven miles, so named to distinguish it from its smaller sister islands of Little Cayman and Cayman Brac). It was an important case, involving substantial contractor's claims and employer's counterclaims concerning an upmarket set of beachfront condominiums.

The proceedings were being conducted on a formal basis. I usually leave it up to the parties, especially where counsel is involved, to determine their own level of informality or otherwise, provided they stay within bounds of judicial decency and conform to the rules of natural justice. In some cases of total formality, or where one party requests, the arbitrator may be required to make a formal declaration of impartiality, ability and so on (see practice note 11). In this case, both sides were represented by counsel and assistants, with all the usual paraphernalia. I recognized Conrad's name from the list of witnesses presented by the claimant and looked forward to seeing him once again after a long absence.

After having given my consent for the witness to be presented, the door burst open, and in stormed Mr Rutkovsky! No diffident entry with a courteous bow to the bench for him. Seeing me, he lurched forward, as in a rugby scrum, skilfully dodging his handler, and extended his hand while loudly exclaiming, "Maurice, you old dog! How nice to see you! How are you? Long time . . . !"

In the face of this unseemly onslaught, I winced, gritted my teeth and, with difficulty, asked his attorney to escort his witness to the witness table. There he sat, still grinning broadly, while the rest of the participants settled down, waiting for me to make the next move.

"Mr X," I began, addressing counsel, "kindly find out if your witness is ready to take the oath or to be affirmed" (see practice note 12). Without waiting for a response, my old friend Conrad rose slowly to his feet and told everyone present, "Look! You know how many years he knows me?

I don't need to be affirmed or oathed. I always speak the truth – don't I, Maurice?"

While never one to be a stickler for formality, this, I decided, was taking informality too far. Assuming my stern arbitrator's face, I addressed counsel and advised him that the decorum of the witness was the complete responsibility of the instructing attorney, and accordingly, I expected him to do his duty. Mr Rutkovsky was admonished, settled down, gave his evidence and was cross-examined and then re-examined, responding as obediently as he was able. Later, after I had politely thanked him for attending, he left. Ultimately his evidence proved to be not of great importance, nor was it used to any great extent by his legal team, but the episode had certainly enlivened the otherwise dull proceedings.

Incidentally, among the joys of Grand Cayman, not too far from Jamaica, is its incredible unspoiled marine life and habitats. Being an arbitrator of the more conscientious kind, my duties always require me to make a thorough and complete inspection of the *locus in quo*, involving much research time on the beach and snorkelling inside the reef. All, I was happy to report, were in perfect judicial order.

I have found not only that it is advisable for an arbitrator to hold a preliminary meeting (see practice note 13), but that if such a meeting is comprehensive and anticipatory, it may be the most important one he will hold in the course of the proceedings. Here will be set out the particular rights and duties of both the parties and the arbitrator that are not covered by the law or by the standard set of arbitration rules the parties (guided by the arbitrator) have adopted (see practice note 10). Of particular importance during the preliminary meeting is the Programme of Service of Pleadings during the interlocutory period – namely, the schedule of formalities each party puts forward in support of their individual cases. Not to be overlooked is also the matter, preferably determined early on in the appointment process, of the arbitrator's fees and charges (see practice note 34).

One item on the agenda for the preliminary meeting is usually related to the giving of evidence under oath. Apart from the usual questions, I always ask if the witness believes in a Supreme Being – and if so, whether it is in accordance with Christianity, Judaism, Islam and so forth. In the rare instance of a witness being an agnostic or atheist, they may give evidence under affirmation of the veracity of their statements.

Over the years, I have hardly ever received objections from a prospective witness to the use of a holy book in the oath. Except recently. Without citing any names, since the action in question is recent, it went as follows:

> Me: "Mr X, kindly request your witness to take the Holy Book in his hand, and repeat after me . . ."
> Witness: "What is this?"
> Me: "It is a Bible – the Old and the New Testaments. Did your counsel not advise you about taking an oath?"
> Witness: "No! Is it Christian or something else? I am Jewish . . ."

I immediately recognized the problem. The witness, being neither Jamaican nor evidently very worldly, was unaware that there was any bible other than the Old Testament, and therefore leery of the book suddenly thrust at him. Summoning the modicum of my knowledge of the language of the Old Testament from my brief sojourn in Israel during the 1950s, I lost patience and barked at him: "*Tikach et ha sefer hazeh, yesh tannach havatique – hacol b'seder achshav! – Kach et zeh!*"

My eldest son (another by-product, incidentally, of my brief sojourn in Israel, and now a professional Hebrew translator) tells me that my Hebrew in this case was by no means flawless. It was, however, good enough to convey to the dumbfounded man in the holy language and in no uncertain terms to *take the book!*, for he responded by mutely extending his hand, into which I thrust the Bible and proceeded to administer the oath in the normal way. The rest of those present were seemingly equally impressed, and the arbitration thereafter proceeded normally.

Not all arbitrators, I hasten to add, possess multiple linguistic talents, and nor do I – I was simply lucky in this instance. It also came in handy during another arbitration, when a tall Rastafarian subcontractor witness, bedecked in full green, gold and black regalia, dreadlocks partly concealed beneath a tall turban, and reeking of a well-known illegal vegetable substance that was then illegal to possess even in small quantities – was reassured by me that the book he was asked to grasp was indeed a faithful translation of the original Holy Scripture, and contained nothing disrespectful of the King of Kings, Conquering Lion of Judah, His Imperial Majesty Hailie Selassie, direct (though long-deceased) representative of the Almighty on earth. Thus assured by me, he proceeded to give his evidence in a most lucid Jamaican fashion.

All of which goes to show that, as an arbitrator, one should not hesitate to fully utilize such skills or experience as one may acquire in life, when applicable, to facilitate proceedings.

3.

St Lucia

St Lucia is a delightful "small" island (as defined by the inhabitants of the larger islands of Jamaica or Trinidad) – only about 230 square miles in size – situated in the Eastern Caribbean, between Barbados and Martinique. Unlike most other, now-independent Caribbean islands that have retained the culture of their former British rulers, St Lucia – having been fought over and alternately occupied innumerable times by Britain and France between the seventeenth and nineteenth centuries – although predominately British in flavour, still retains strong traces of French influence in its culture and language.

As with most of the Commonwealth Caribbean, in the wake of greater accessibility – or in the case of the super-rich, the greater exclusivity – afforded by jet travel, St Lucia has had its share of the questionable benefit of explosive growth in tropical tourism. One such destination is the site of the Jalousie Plantation Resort and Spa, located south of the town of Soufrière on the southwest coast of the island. Long before it was chosen for a hotel development, this location was a well-known point of interest and site of natural beauty, bounded as it was on either side by two cone-shaped peaks known as Gros Piton and Petit Piton. In between lies the beach, which, unlike its counterparts in most tourist brochures, is remarkable for not being the expected white or golden, but rather dark grey in colour, due to the volcanic character of this part of the island. Oh, and also for its elephant.

The majestic pachyderm in question was a pet of the site's original owner, an eccentric and entertaining English aristocrat known to all as Lord Glenconner. The title was no nickname or affectation: he was, to be precise, the third Baron Glenconner (the first being his grandfather, a Liberal member of Parliament who was elevated to the House of Lords in 1911). Lord Glenconner's daily exercise regime consisted of a morning and evening walk with the elephant from one end of the beach to the other. A small, thin, brown local boy, christened "Sabu", sat between the ears of the animal and assisted with the steering. This walk was followed by breakfast or cocktails, respectively (for Lord Glenconner, that is – not the elephant). His Lordship had recently sold the site to a wealthy and well-connected Middle Eastern family, and, at our first meeting on the construction site, informed us that his close friend Her Royal Highness Princess Margaret was fond of visiting the adjoining island of Mustique – which he had purchased in 1958 – and popping over now and again for drinks. We were suitably impressed.

My involvement in the dispute, which had emerged following construction of the proposed Jalousie Plantation Resort and Spa at the site in question, was not as arbitrator. That role was fulfilled by Dr John Uff, a highly distinguished English lawyer and arbitrator and, at the time, also Professor of Engineering and Construction Law at King's College in London. In May 1993, I was contacted by a large prestigious firm of attorneys in Miami, inviting me to join their team in representing the site's current owners. The firm's letterhead boasted half a dozen names of Eastern European origin and one Anglo-Saxon one – a Mr Brooks – who, I assumed, was also its only non-Jewish partner. When we met in Miami, I discovered that he was not only a co-religionist, but also avuncular, jovial and highly knowledgeable to boot.

Before being briefed in the attorneys' sumptuous, modern offices in downtown Miami, I was put through a most interesting cross-cultural judicial experience. Mr Brooks began by admitting scant knowledge of the process of arbitration in general, and even less of the mystical vagaries of British court practice, which, he correctly surmised, roughly applied to arbitrations as well. His traditional approach to court matters, he explained – which, he assumed, applied to arbitrations too – was based on the principle of attack first: go for the jugular; then, if anything is left of the opponent, assess one's next move. For my part, I confessed that my knowledge of his domain was limited to what I had learned from watching court dramas on American TV. I was also aware, if not of the details, certainly of the broad differences between the two approaches with regard to attaining justice, or at least a successful outcome, for one's client. It was a two-way learning experience that I enjoyed tremendously. It went well until the last part, where we had great difficulty reconciling our two stylistic approaches to presenting evidence. Mine, steeped in the tradition of subtlety, allegory and respect, was diametrically opposed to his aggressive, almost bullying (it seemed to me) methods of persuading a jury or judge. Eventually, however, I managed to convince him that the arbitrator, Dr Uff, would adversely react to his style of presentation and, conversely, appreciate my assistance in preparing a Scott Schedule to assist the proceedings (see practice notes 18 and 19). In return, Mr Brooks and his legal assistant succeeded in ridding me of some of my typically British (or Caribbean) inclination to self-effacing turns of speech, persuading me to be, if not more aggressive, at least more emphatic in my oral delivery.

A harmonious and symbiotic professional relationship having been established to the satisfaction of both parties, we broke for lunch at a nearby Cuban restaurant, where I was given a little background on the case (and, I should add, the best example of highly spiced Cuban-style cooked oxtail and beans I have ever had, before or since).The clients, I was told, were an important Middle Eastern oil family with close ties to the ruler (as all such families seem to have in that part of the globe). The said ruler (for convenience henceforth referred to as the "employer") had entered into an informal agreement with a particular firm of Brazilian contractors to build a multibillion US-dollar water project in the mountainous region of the employer's country, adjoining Azerbaijan (then still part of the Soviet Union). Although no binding contract had yet been signed, the contractors claimed that they had been promised that as soon as the project's details were included in a treaty between the employer's country and its neighbour, the contract would be theirs.

As happens in these instances, and as the attorney's assistant continued, the said treaty was taking a little longer to finalize than expected. This meant that although the contractor had partially mobilized in anticipation of the construction, no contract could be signed, and the contractor was asked to stand by. In the meantime, as a gesture of goodwill to compensate for this inconvenience, the employer offered them a small contract to build this resort in St Lucia. Agreeing, the Brazilian contractor dispatched his senior representatives to St Lucia, with instructions to build the hotel and return as soon as possible and in time for the larger project in the Middle East.

The briefing now over – or so I thought – all I desired after that magnificent lunch was to take my usual post-lunch siesta. Instead, our team leader led us back to his office at a brisk pace to complete the session. This consisted mainly of my telling the attorneys how I visualized the arbitrator would receive the rather amateurishly prepared statements of the other side and how, conversely, he would be impressed by the detailed, priced and described bills of quantities (a process unfamiliar to my American colleagues) that my office in Kingston would prepare in support of our client's counterclaims. Once this and other details had been finalized, I was finally released from the glass skyscraper confines of Mr Brooks et al., to return to my hotel and thence to Kingston.

I will not bore you with the administrative details of preparations for the actual arbitration, mostly exchanges of documents, discovery and other interlocutory matters, which were conducted in London) (see practice note 14). In the balance of the hearing, following a short interval – agreed by the parties because of the many possible locations – the seat of the arbitration (see practice note 37) was agreed to be St Lucia. Consequently the hearings would be held in situ at the hotel in St Lucia.

The journey from Kingston to St Lucia was not nearly as comfortable as the flight to Miami had been: the main airline then serving the Caribbean region was BWIA, or British West Indian Airlines – a pompous title for a rather uncomfortable and unreliable carrier (cynics claimed the acronym stood for Britain's Worst Investment Abroad). To get to St Lucia then from Jamaica, one flew from Kingston to Barbados, transferred to an even smaller, propeller-driven aircraft that flew with fits and starts, arriving eventually at one's destination. Fortunately, as a veteran Caribbean resident by that point, I was not too inconvenienced by this, and since the route was well travelled by members of the University of the West Indies, which has campuses in Jamaica, Barbados and Trinidad, there were plenty of enjoyable conversations to be had en route.

The hotel, I observed on arrival, was nearly completed. I was not overly impressed with the architecture, its layout on the site or the finishings, but it was at a sufficiently advanced stage of construction to accommodate all of us who had gathered for the arbitration.

After settling down, we were summoned to the office of the owner's representative, his son. The office, which had been prepared for him in advance of his occasional visits to the site, was fairly large, and furnished in keeping with the status of its occupant. As one entered, one could not escape noticing, behind the grand executive desk, a wall-to-wall photograph of a handsome young man – olive complexion, his upper lip weighed down by a lush black moustache – clearly the same gentleman who graciously rose to greet us, fully kitted out and about to take off in an F-16 fighter aircraft. Although I was sure we were all curious, I was the only one who had the temerity to ask the young man if the pilot in the picture was indeed him. Flattered and grinning, he nodded. Needing no further prompting, he explained:

"Yes, it was taken a few years ago – it was a twenty-first birthday gift from the Emir, my father. It was surplus: we bought it from the US Marines and decided that since, for many reasons, I would not be able to fly it full-out at home – as I love to do in Arizona – I should keep it in the States, for when I visit. Beautiful, isn't she?"

In reply I remember mumbling something about second-hand F-16s losing their value on a trade-in. My weak attempt at humour was greeted, predictably, with silence.

The young prince entertained us royally that evening and the following day. And though we never saw him at the hotel again, before he left he made the necessary arrangements for our stay to be as comfortable as possible in terms of the rooms and generous meals and refreshments.

In keeping with British arbitral practice, throughout the hearings the arbitrator refrained from dining with us or the other side's representatives, to preserve his position of neutrality, as well as reminding participants of the general principle of confidentiality (see practice note 20).

The hearing itself was a tribute to Dr Uff's judicial skills in diplomatically handling the witnesses and the presentation of evidence (see practice note 38). He conducted the proceedings firmly but fairly, with due regard to the multilingual nature of the case: English (including American English), Portuguese and St Lucian patois. As I sat listening to the evidence presented, it occurred to me that the proceedings were a reflection of how the construction project had been run by the contractors. Brazilian tradesmen or subcontractors gave evidence, which was translated from Portuguese to Standard English. Instructions were then further refined on-site, and information was conveyed in the patois of the local workmen. The Brazilian contractors must have had great difficulty in conveying their requirements to the St Lucian masons and carpenters, but the reverse was probably also true. The results, I concluded, must have bordered on the hilarious, if not the disastrous.

As far as the evidence was concerned, I was happy that I had insisted, in my pre-trial discussions with Mr Brooks and his cohorts, that traditional quantity surveying techniques and forms of presentations be used in supporting the attorneys' legal arguments. Indeed, I am sure that this was the primary contributing factor to our ultimate success. The evidence of the other side was emotional, unstructured and, unlike ours, unrelated to the original contract. Indeed, the only "expert" witness (see practice note 17) they produced was a brash Texan who produced quotations from authors of English arbitral texts with which I had worked in other cases. Dressed in a garish necktie and bright green blazer, the Texan flashed his gold Rolex at every opportunity as part of a general flamboyant display. The arbitrator was kind and allowed his testimony to continue despite his absolute destruction under cross-examination. By contrast, the meticulous work that my office in Kingston had prepared was accepted as real evidence and referred to extensively by the arbitrator in his award (see practice note 23).

The hearings now concluded, we could finally relax: a swim and piña coladas poolside were in order. No sooner had the sun began casting its setting shadow, however, than who should appear – clad in long-sleeved white shirt, his trademark soccer referee whistle suspended from his neck – but Lord Glenconner himself. After we'd exchanged greetings, he replied to our first question about the conspicuous absence of his elephant by informing us how impractical it had been to keep such a pet once the hotel was built, and how he had therefore reluctantly shipped Sabu and him off to a circus in the Dominican Republic. On the bright side, he revealed that on the stretch of beach that he had retained, adjoining the hotel, he had built a rum bar, to which we were all cordially invited after dinner, for drinks and . . . whatnot. In a bid, no doubt, to impress those of us who had not heard the story before, he apologized for the absence of Her Royal Highness, who – he was at pains to point out – continued to be a frequent visitor to his haunt, and he to hers, on nearby Mustique.

In bright moonlight, and fully unwound now that the tension of the arbitration of the past few weeks was over, we all trooped down the beach to His Lordship's rustic premises. Fires had been lit on the beach – for effect as well as to keep the mosquitoes away – a local mento band was in full swing and local couples were dancing languidly to the tropical beat. As soon as we arrived, our host strode towards us blowing long blasts of greeting on his whistle. Rum punch was the drink of the night, mixed in a large pan. No glass was allowed to remain empty for even a moment – any thus sighted was announced by a long blast of the whistle, whereupon all glasses were immediately refilled. No record exists of the remainder of the proceedings. Suffice it to say, we were all present and accounted for early next morning.

Judging by the conversations at breakfast before departure the next day, not a great deal was remembered of the night before – or if it was, it was not spoken of. Bags were packed, and taxis waited, and we bade our fond farewells to each other and to the hotel as we planned to return to reality, to await the publication of Dr Uff's arbitration award.

In August 1995, it finally arrived and, as we had hoped, confirmed that our client had been successful. It was a reasoned, interim award, in the sense that it awaited his final decision on costs. One of the arbitrator's comments, in particular, on the subject of the contract was interesting:

> The contract between the parties was made in unconventional circumstances and in an unusual manner, which is also reflected in a number of difficulties inherent in the contract documents themselves. . . . In the summer of 1989, after a substantial period of planning and pre-selection of tenderers, the project was offered to four international contractors on conventional tendering documents. The lowest of these, Contractor X, submitted a tender of approximately US$15.9 million. The Claimant was not one of the tenderers.

The remainder of the award quoted extensively from my analyses and bills of quantities and was used by the arbitrator to assess the relative values of his award. Although we heard nothing more about the noble baron, or his elephant, we were well pleased with the outcome.

4.

Mr Isaacs

Not all arbitrations are grand or exotic – in fact, most are minor and mundane – but arbitrators, as I always remind the parties involved in my hearings, must constantly be aware of their social responsibility and use whatever skills and experience they may have for the benefit of those seeking their services. So it was in the case of one Mr Isaacs, a recently retired Jamaican civil servant who had purchased a small two-storey, one-bedroom house in a new housing development on top of Long Mountain overlooking eastern Kingston.

For centuries, this site had been the verdant green watershed area for the eastern half of the parish of Kingston and St Andrew, serving the Mona reservoir on the mountain's western flank. Now, thanks to the growing need at the lower end of the housing market for mass-produced units of this kind and the laidback attitude of the authorities towards all things ecological, Mr Isaacs was the proud owner of one of the units in this project.

It appears that he had really wanted a two-bedroom house to accommodate his recently graduated daughter, his wife and himself, but the developers apparently had only obtained planning consent for the house as built, hence his immediate need for a small two-storey extension to contain the additional bedroom on the upper floor and provide slightly more space to the kitchen on the ground level. Mr Isaacs was not the only buyer in the project to have been faced with this dilemma upon taking possession of a unit. Fortunately, the project's developers had, with foresight and economic initiative, anticipated this need and produced standard plans and estimates for such proposed extensions. These might not have passed the scrutiny of the planning authorities had they been presented before consent was granted, but this being Jamaica in the year 2004, expediency prevailed.

Contracts were signed for Mr Isaacs's extension, and work was begun by crews that had no problems, since it had already become a repetitive exercise. A short while later Mr Isaacs and his daughter (we never did see his wife, for some strange reason) settled into their new quarters.

All of this, you understand, was gleaned by me through subsequent evidence and testimonies of witnesses who were only too happy to share their unfortunate experiences with the developers, contractors and other equally alleged menaces to society involved in the Long Mountain project.

At the hearing, both sides duly turned up, each represented by counsel who replied to my standard question as to whether there were any legal issues (see practice note 39) that needed settling before I get involved on a technical basis. Both assured me that there were none, following which a site visit was arranged for all of us to view the problems. To expedite pro-ceedings and save time, I suggested having the hearing held *in situ*, and the parties agreed.

We duly arrived at the Isaacs' residence and assembled in the living room, with barely space enough for those present to turn around. I conducted whatever semi-formal proceedings I considered necessary and received the oral pleadings of both parties. First, the claimant's list of alleged defects was presented. Most were immensely trivial and only some actually appeared on the points of claim, but in the spirit of natural justice, they received as much attention as if they were of great moral, financial and legal significance, until we finally arrived at the main issue: the leaking roof. After acceding to the claimant's request that we all remove our shoes (a religious or fastidious requirement, I knew not which), we trooped up the narrow staircase, one at a time, to view faint water stains at the junction of the wall and roof. I agreed that this indeed indicated the possibility of water penetration and that the only way to be sure was to inspect the roof covering from the outside. With the consensus of all present, we trooped back downstairs, re-donned our shoes and went outside the building to be shown by Mr Isaacs the only point of access to the roof, which was situated on top of a sixteen-foot-high, blank wall. Since this was the rear wall of the extension, and built almost at the boundary of the lot, I guessed the top of the wall to be over a hundred feet above street level.

It was a daunting prospect, but since it was my suggestion and so as not to lose face, I had no choice but to ask for a ladder. None was available.

"But you are the arbitrator," replied Mr Isaacs. "Why did you not bring one with you?"

"I apologize for that obvious oversight," said I defensively, somewhat taken aback by the uncharacteristic expression of assertiveness by the mild-mannered Mr Isaacs. "Perhaps you can get one or borrow one so that we may jointly get onto the roof?"

"No! I don't know any of my neighbors, and if I have to get a ladder, I'll have to rent one. And who's going to pay for that, may I ask?" he replied indignantly.

I glanced at his attorney for some kind of help or support, but none was forthcoming. As sole arbitrator, this was a moment of truth: not one upon which my entire reputation hinged, perhaps, but certainly one that called for a demonstration of some authority on my part.

Some ten days later, I heard from Mr Isaacs that he had identified a source of ladder rental. We agreed on a mutually convenient date for my ascent and met on the appointed day. The ladder – a rather flimsy affair, I thought – was already in place on my arrival, leaning against the wall.

Mr Isaacs went first. Being comparatively slight in build and, I assumed, having tested the ladder before my arrival, he clambered up with the apparent ease of someone who did this sort of thing often. After waiting for him to reach the top, and with a great deal of trepidation, I gingerly followed, not daring to look down at the cars below that appeared much smaller than they ought. With gritted teeth and great concern for my grandchildren, who might now unexpectedly and tragically find themselves minus one grandfather, I eventually made my way up and climbed over the parapet to join Mr Isaacs on the roof. We proceeded to inspect the roof coverings and flashings in question, until, at the earliest opportunity that seemed decent, I declared satisfaction at the extent of the inspection and suggested we return. This time I went first and, again trying desperately not to look down to the street below, gratefully returned to terra firma.

Shortly afterwards I issued my brief award in favour of Mr Isaacs. It ordered certain specified remedial works to be carried out by the contractors within a specified time frame. I took care to include the cost of the ladder rental in my award of costs (see practice note 42).

5.

Me and the House of Lords

There are still, in Jamaica, many fine examples of Georgian architecture, not necessarily attributable to our great record of historic preservation, but simply because there was so much of it to begin with. During the British colonial period, and as a result of the benefit of the profitable sugar industry, many Georgian residences and municipal buildings were erected, most of them faithful to the basic principles of the architecture of the period by virtue of copying designs in books of English origin.

Montego Bay was fortunate in having one such landmark structure in the form of the parish capital courthouse, with lower-storey walls of cut limestone supporting a timber-framed and -clad upper floor and a timber-framed pitched roof covered with local cedar shingles. It served the people and its purpose for well over two centuries, until, one fateful night in the 1970s, a fire destroyed the entire building, leaving only the external stone walls. The building remained in this derelict condition for several years, an eyesore in the most prominent position in Sam Sharpe Square (formerly Charles Square). Some said, "Good riddance to a memorial to colonial slavery", while others regretted the cultural loss. In the end, it was decided that the government would reconstruct the court house at the same site, restoring the original external appearance but building a modern set of municipal offices and other facilities inside.

The Urban Development Corporation (UDC) in Kingston, fulfilling their mandate to give employment to the local (Montego Bay) architects but knowing the project was too large for any one of the one-man firms then practising in Montego Bay, appointed two firms jointly to prepare the reconstruction plans: Harold Simpson Associates (Architects) Limited and the Michael Carter Partnership. Both architects were old acquaintances of mine. Carter, the younger of the two, had originally arrived in Jamaica as an expatriate to work for the Ministry of Housing, and later moved to Montego Bay to start his own office. Simpson was already established as an architect in Montego Bay when I worked there in the early 1960s: a slim, bald Scotsman, and a contemporary of my old boss, Jim Mitchell. My association with both architects was both casual and amicable.

In accordance with UDC requirements, the two architects entered into a joint-venture agreement to provide architectural services for the construction of a proposed Montego Bay Civic Centre, as it was to be known, and began working together in late 1994. The agreement had two clauses of interest: one regarding the sharing of fees, and the other, an arbitration clause to be invoked in the case of any irreconcilable differences that might occur in the execution of their contract.

Inevitably, partly because of the vast personality differences between the two and partly because of Simpson's sudden illness, disputes arose over money, and the arbitration clause was duly invoked. By that time, I had developed a minor reputation as an arbitrator in the building industry, and so, being known to both complainants but having no connection with either one, in December 1997 I was duly appointed as the sole arbitrator to settle the matters in dispute. Both parties retained legal counsel: for Simpson (the claimant), Ms Carol Davis of the Kingston firm of Davis, Bennett and Beecher–Bravo; and for Carter (the respondent), Mr Ripton Macpherson, CD, JP, of the Montego Bay firm of Ripton Macpherson and Company.

In keeping with my normal practice, I held a preliminary meeting with all interested parties present (including, for reasons unknown to me, the then member of Parliament for the constituency and civil engineer, Mr Arthur Nelson). The meeting spelled out my requirements for the conduct of the arbitration and a timeline for the proceedings. Because of the lack of suitable premises to accommodate all the parties and witnesses involved, I prevailed upon the good offices of my old and dear friend Tony Hart, who secured for us the use of the conference room at the Montego Bay Yacht Club. A more bucolic and comfortable environment within which to conduct such proceedings would be hard to imagine. The room overlooked the yacht basin adjoining the harbour, with an ever-changing vista of elegant and languid sailing boats plying the crystal-clear waters of the azure-blue Caribbean Sea. Needless to say, the arbitrator's chair was, once again, the one with the view.

The hearings were duly conducted with presentations by both sides, witnesses called, examined and cross-examined, until their uneventful conclusion in early September 1998 following closing addresses (see practice notes 21 and 22) to me by both parties. After deliberating and drafting the award (see practice notes 24, 25 and 26), I handed it down on the twenty-third of that month in favour of the claimant, Harold Simpson Associates (Architects) Limited, with costs awarded against the respondent. I was happy that the matter had been settled, and pleased that it had been accomplished in such pleasant surroundings and without any evident acrimony on the part of the respondent. How wrong I was.

On 12 September 1999, the *Sunday Gleaner*, a local newspaper, reported that the respondent, through his attorney Mr Ripton Macpherson, had appealed to the Supreme Court to set aside my award, on the grounds that "there . . . was an error on the face of the Award".

On 7 February 1999, Justice Lloyd Ellis of the Supreme Court allowed the appeal, agreeing with the respondent that there was indeed an error on the face of the award. He further commented:

> There is in the award a plethora of references to the joint venture agreement. The question is: are those references indicia of incorporation. I so find that they are and that there has been an incorporation of agreement into the award [see practice note 31].
>
> Having found that, it is true to say that I am entitled to look at the agreement. When I do so, I have a strong suspicion that the arbitrator erred in not dealing with matters as it relates specifically to clause 4.01 which deals with profits.
>
> The award was in relation to fees; I agree with Mr Morrison (counsel for the Respondents) that there was an error on the face. That error vitiates the award and leads to the conclusion that the award has to be set aside.

In response – the *Gleaner* report continued – Harold Simpson appealed against the Supreme Court ruling on the grounds that there was in fact no error on the face of the award.

Unfortunately, having handed down my award – correct or not – by law, my position now was nothing more than that of a bystander (or to use the legal Latin phrase, *functus officio*). I no longer had any role to play in these subsequent matters, except to hope that eventually I would be vindicated and my reputation restored.

In the Court of Appeal of the Jamaican Supreme Court (Nos. 75 & 76/00, 9 & 97/01), the learned judges were asked to determine whether there was, or was not, an error on the face of my award, and, if so, whether it should be set aside. After due deliberation, the esteemed panel found that my award was in fact correct, for the following reasons:

> The Joint Venture Agreement was not incorporated in the award and the trial judge was not permitted to roam through its contents in search of a place to anchor his findings that there was an error on the face of the award.
>
> The court allowed the appeal, set aside the judgement of Justice Ellis and reinstated the award of the arbitrator. The costs of the appeal and the trial were awarded to Harold Simpson Associates.

Hearing this, I breathed a huge sigh of relief. Sadly, poor Harold Simpson himself was unable to savour the taste of success, since he had recently suffered serious injuries in a road accident in Montego Bay.

As I have learned so many times in my career, however, "It ain't over till the fat lady sings." In this case the fat lady was English and comprised the Law Lords of the Judicial Committee of the Privy Council of the House of Lords. Mr Carter and his legal counsel were not ready to call it quits; they were not content with the ruling of the Jamaican Court of Appeal, and now sought the opinion of the highest court in the British Commonwealth in a last-ditch attempt to achieve an elusive victory. We speculated on Mr Carter's ability to afford the huge expense of mounting such an appeal. Had he been advised to seek third-party funding (see practice note 35)? Was some kind of strategy involved? Certainly at this late stage, and especially given that Mr Simpson had not yet shown any signs of recovery from his injuries and illness, we, in the interest of natural justice, were not about to let one side succeed for want of interest or resources of the other side to support its case in the coming appeal.

The eventual judgement of the Privy Council – specifically Lord Hoffman,

Lord Hope of Craighead, Lord Scott of Foscote, Lord Rodgers of Earlsferry and Dame Sian Elias – was handed down on 14 June 2004 (Privy Council Appeal No. 27 of 2003). It is a model of clear English. With the utmost brevity and legal erudition, they summarized the issues, tracing the legal history of applicable precedents as far as 1851, with the ultimate conclusion that I was correct in my conduct of the arbitration, and that Justice Ellis was wrong in his overturning and condemnation of my award. In summary, they stated, the appeal failed completely, and my original award must stand as published by me. In their final words, their Lordships concluded with the following statement: "Their Lordships will therefore humbly advise Her Majesty that the appeals should be dismissed with costs."

Under normal circumstances, the news would have been cause for celebratory rounds of champagne. However, in Montego Bay in particular, it was received in sombre silence, because in the interim, poor Harry Simpson had succumbed to his injuries and passed away.

6.

Bonaire

Strictly speaking, this is not an arbitration story. Well, in a way it is, but in any event, I could not resist telling of one of the most impressive sights on any Caribbean island that I have ever come across in my professional career. The island in question is one of the famous Dutch colonial ABC Islands – Aruba, Bonaire and Curaçao – lying some fifty miles off the north coast of Venezuela.

One day – sometime in the early 1970s, I believe – I received a call from the station manager of KLM Royal Dutch Airlines in Kingston. If I was not too busy, could I visit their offices downtown to discuss a matter of assistance to them?

At the meeting downtown I was quickly briefed: the airline owned the major hotel in Bonaire, the operators of which wanted to embark upon a major construction expansion to cash in on what they perceived to be an impending tourist boom. The airline, being less certain of future revenues and more conservative, needed an impartial opinion from me on two points: a) whether what was being proposed by the present hotel operators was a feasible proposition, and b) whether the construction costs submitted by the local operators were correct and in line with local and international pricing levels.

Needing little prompting, I packed my bag, patted my two young children on their heads, and kissed my wife au revoir. After a rather uncomfortable hop, skip and bump from one island to another, I eventually found myself in the delightful tropical version of a Dutch village in the subtropical setting of Bonaire, and, courtesy of the airline, I was whisked away to the hotel to recover.

As I normally do when in a new and unknown place for the first time, I immediately proceeded to find out about the island. Geographically, it is boomerang-shaped, averaging five miles wide and twenty-four miles long, fairly flat, the highest point being the hill in one of the two national parks at each extremity of the island, at about 750 feet high. The history of the island is also interesting in that their original indigenous population was the same as that of Jamaica and many other Caribbean islands, Arawaks or Taíno – peaceful peoples who, in the centuries before the Spanish conquest, were decimated by the aggressive and warlike Caribs. The first Europeans set foot in Bonaire a little later than in Jamaica – 1499, I was told – and, as in Jamaica, moved on, since they found no gold there. This made it easier for the ABC islands to be acquired by the Dutch in 1633, some twenty-two years before England (under Cromwell) seized Jamaica from the Spanish.

Bonaire is the most easterly of the three sister islands – Aruba being the westerly and Curaçao in the middle. The three share much of the same history, with Curaçao having the added distinction of hosting one of the oldest Jewish settlements in the western hemisphere (if not *the* oldest). These were Spanish Jews who, fleeing the Spanish Inquisition after 1492, landed in Portuguese Brazil – in particular, in Recife on the eastern coast, this being the shortest distance across the Atlantic. Once the Portuguese Inquisition reached Brazil too, the Jewish escapees fled north from Recife, finding refuge first in Curaçao and then farther north, in Jamaica, St Thomas and, in some cases, even as far as Charleston and New Amsterdam (New York) in the English colonies of North America.

Next, mainly from taxi drivers and hotel staff, I discovered the local patois, which to the untrained ear sounds at first like a bouillabaisse of all known languages mixed together. And that is very nearly true. *Papiamentu* – to give it its correct name – is a mixture of African (via the slave trade), Portuguese (from the refugees from Brazil), Arawak Indian, Spanish and Dutch – with English and French subsequently added to the mix, not unlike Jamaican Patois. Handed down from generation to generation, it had, I was informed by the hotel manager, no written language. All of this I found absolutely fascinating and a legitimate part of my "research" into the underlying culture of the then fledgling tourist industry.

Continuing my quest, and with the help of friendly taxi drivers, I visited construction sites and spoke – as well as I could – to workers and supervisors, to get a feel of the basic cost of building materials and productivity of tradesmen, construction methods and so on. I had done this before in other places in the region successfully, to determine the local construction costs in relation to the US dollar and various other currencies. Once I had established the cost of local wages and materials, I would then visit the local supermarket and check the cost of a "basket" of imported and local produce. With prices already recorded by me from supermarkets in Miami, and by interpolating those results to proven prices from competitive tenders in Jamaica, I was able to come up with a fairly accurate comparative table of elemental construction costs. Years later – in 1986 – *The Economist* magazine did much the same with its initially tongue-in-cheek "Big Mac Index", comparing the prices of a sample basket of goods in various countries in terms of local buying power instead of official exchange rates. My results varied little from those arrived at scientifically or electronically.

In the meantime, I was being wined and dined by the senior management of the hotel and of the airline. At first, I had ethical pangs of conscience. How could I accept such offerings and, at the same time, both as a quantity surveyor and as a kind of mediator/arbitrator, remain completely objective? I solved my ethical dilemma by either drinking the champagne alone, or insisting that our dinners, at various restaurants chosen by my hosts, be taken in the presence of both parties to the enquiry – the airline and the hotel.

After about a week of viewing the industry from the top down, and, as it were, from the bottom up, and with the recent successful Jamaican hotel expansion in mind, I had more or less made up my mind that Bonaire's tourist industry was indeed ready for great expansion. As I would subsequently state in my report, the hotel expansion was undoubtedly a good idea.

By that time, I had seen most of the island, with the exception of their famous salt pans at its southern tip; this, my co-hosts told me, would be, as it were, and not mixing metaphors, the icing on the cake. Accordingly, on the day before my scheduled departure, I was provided with a car, a driver and a young woman tour guide to accompany my visit to them. Reminding my hosts of my wish to preserve impartiality, this imbalance was promptly solved by the airline sending another attractive tour guide to accompany us – an amicable arrangement that raised no further arbitral objections from me.

Salt, as King Lear learned the hard way, is one of the essential staples of life. In the ancient world, it was considered so precious a commodity that it was used to pay the wages of Roman legionnaires (hence the word *salary*).

Apart from salt mining, the oldest method of obtaining salt is from the sea, by evaporation. In the seventeenth century, in a bid to provide their motherland with alternative sources of salt after Portugal was taken over by Spain, Dutch settlers in Bonaire began producing salt by digging innumerable salt pans at the flat end of the island – each about two or three acres in size – surrounded by earthwork mounds to keep in the water during evaporation. This being well before the era of industrial machinery, excavations were carried out by hand by the enslaved Africans imported to work on the cane plantations, who were further made to harvest the salt for export to other islands and for sale to the buccaneers roaming the region. Today, the salt pans are still in production, under private ownership.

Viewing the blinding whiteness of the vast expanse of the salt pans must be like seeing a lunar landscape close up. They stretch for acres from one coastline to the other and from their northern end to the sea at the southern tip of the peninsula. Their unbroken, pristine whiteness is astounding, and today, they are one of the island's chief tourist attractions. At the time of my visit, the area was closed to the public, because it was the mating season of the transitory flamingoes. Fortuitously, my hosts had obtained special permission for us to enter.

Some eight thousand pink flamingoes waded elegantly to and fro in the salt pans. This, I was told, was one of the few such breeding grounds for pink flamingoes in the world, and the population fluctuated between seven and fifteen thousand, depending on the season. (Today, I have been told, the number is around forty thousand.) The sight of this multitude of vivid pink flamingoes set against a white backdrop was one I shall never forget, and in itself was enough to make the trip worthwhile.

After I had completed my assignment in Bonaire, my hosts gave me a fond send-off into the sunset. In Kingston, my report was duly prepared – minus descriptions of female tour guides, flamingoes and Papiamentu – and transmitted to KLM, which gave the go-ahead for the hotel expansion.

7.

Antigua

In this region, qualified arbitrators – especially those with a modicum of practical experience and knowledge of West Indian matters and culture – are sometimes called upon to use those skills in situations that are not strictly arbitral. Just such a case occurred in August 2001, when I received a fax from the secretary of then vice chancellor Sir Alister McIntyre of the Kingston campus of the University of the West Indies, informing me of the following:

> Sir Alister McIntyre has been appointed by the Government of Antigua and Barbuda to chair a Commission of Enquiry into the operations of a Medical Scheme in that country.
>
> Sir Alister has now asked me to contact you to enquire whether you will be available to undertake an assignment in connection with these investigations which he is conducting. He has advised that the matter is extremely urgent and the assignment would begin immediately and cover a period of about three weeks. The investigator would not necessarily be required to be in Antigua for the entire period of time.
>
> If you are available, I shall be grateful if you will send him, today, a copy of your CV as well as the scales of your fees to the contact number below:
> The Hon. Sir Alister McIntyre
> Royal Antigua Hotel, &c.

I wasted no time in responding. Sir Alister was soon to retire as vice chancellor (to be succeeded by the Honourable Rex Nettleford, my good friend and godfather of my second son). Alister was an old friend, whom I first met in the late 1950s, soon after my arrival in Jamaica. Like most thinking young people at the time, we were actively involved in the politics of the left – especially in Jamaica, which was then still very much a British colony – and in anticipation of the inevitable independence, we met in groups to debate and write about how we saw the future. I was fortunate enough to have been introduced into one such group, known as the New World Group, and I regaled them with my stories about communal life on an Israeli kibbutz, as well as remembered extracts from lectures on Fabian socialism from my adolescence in London. Alister McIntyre was one of that long-forgotten group.

Shortly after receiving my invitation, we met at Jamaica House (the official Office of the Prime Minister), and I was briefed on the commission's work in Antigua. I explained that if I was to be of any real use to Sir Alister and the anticipated public reaction that would inevitably follow the enquiry, my work would have to stand up not only to scrutiny, but possibly also to cross-examination. Hence, I would first need to research basic Antiguan construction costs and other facts, and assemble them in such a way that they could be used in determining the conclusions arrived at. He agreed, and we arranged a date and time for me to meet him and the other two commissioners in St John's, the capital of Antigua.

As with most Caribbean islands, including Jamaica, the aboriginal population of the island were Arawaks, a docile, agricultural folk whose peaceful occupation of the islands over many centuries came to an abrupt and violent end in the late Middle Ages after invasion and possession by the Caribs, an aggressive people that swept across the entire Caribbean. The Caribs' first contact with Europeans was in 1493, when Columbus discovered the island during his second voyage to the region. He named it Santa Maria de la Antigua – after a noted cathedral in Seville, whose name he vowed to give to many of the islands during this voyage. The Caribs put up stiff resistance to the Spaniards, who, finding no fresh water on the island, were willing to leave it mostly to its own devices for over a century and only nominally part of the Spanish Crown.

English settlers, however, colonized the island in 1632, and, shortly after, they introduced sugar cultivation and, subsequently, the evils of the slave trade. By the end of the eighteenth century, Antigua had become an important strategic port as well as a valuable commercial colony. Horatio Nelson –

he of the future Battle of Trafalgar fame – arrived in 1784 and supervised the development of English Harbour as a strategic British naval base. The abolition of slavery here, as throughout the British empire, in 1834 gave a strong boost to the local economy and social climate. Along with the neighbouring island of Barbuda, Antigua gained associated statehood and membership in the Commonwealth in 1967, and full independence in 1981. Political pioneer V.C. Bird became the first prime minister, to be succeeded by his son Lester Bird of the Antigua Labour Party. The main opposition group was then a coalition called the United Progressive Party.

Geographically Antigua is situated roughly in the middle of the Leeward Islands, with Montserrat and Guadaloupe to the south, and St Kitts and St Barts to the west and northwest, respectively. In size, it measures about 14 by 11 miles, approximately 150 square miles (roughly two and a half times the area of Washington, DC). It then hosted a population of about seventy thousand.

After this brief introduction to the history and geography of the island, I was briefed on the objectives of the commission of inquiry. The terms of reference informed me of the following:

> WHEREAS the Governor-General, acting on the advice of the Cabinet, deems it advisable for the public welfare that a Commission should be issued under and by virtue of Section 2 of the Commissions of Inquiry Act, Chapter 91 to inquire into the conduct of the Medical Benefits Scheme . . . and in particular to inquire into the question as to whether there have been any violations of the Medical Benefits Act . . . and the Loans (Mount St John Hospital Construction and Equipping) Act and Standard Accounting Practices.

There followed a comprehensive list of activities for the commission to investigate and report on, including the disbursement of funds; procurement policies, practices, weaknesses and abuses; the overall financing of the construction of a pharmacy building and community clinics; payments to individuals not qualified for benefits under the act; and finally, the overall operations of the Medical Benefits Scheme and recommendations with regard to possible improvement of management.

Sir Alister and one other commission member, Dr John Anthony Roberts, QC, of the United Kingdom, were accommodated in comfortable cottages attached to the hotel. I was put up in a hotel nearby, and a fourth member – a stout, jovial Antiguan by the name of Oscar Frederick, who was appointed as an impartial citizen member of the board – lived locally and visited us occasionally. (As the proceedings drew to a close, I learned that he also harboured political ambitions and that this was a perfect springboard to effect that ambition.)

We were aided in the course of the enquiry by a special legal adviser who would lead our legal team once the public enquiry got underway; he was the former attorney general of Barbados, Dr Richard L. Cheltenham, QC ("Jonny" to his friends). Under the inspired guidance of Sir Alister, we all had separate and specialized functions to perform in this drama and so, in our non-competitive roles, we all got on famously together.

The first day was spent with Sir Alister giving us a detailed mission briefing, lightened by his trademark dry sense of humour, of the background of the Medical Benefits Scheme and the political intrigues and plots surrounding it. Dr Roberts, an experienced Kenyan jurist and a long-standing member of the English bar, was aghast at the tales of nepotism and corruption that appeared to plague the scheme we were about to investigate. The rest of us – all being West Indian – were hardly surprised. Similar stories about other schemes and projects were familiar to us from our own countries (with the possible exception of Barbados), and since by the end of the briefing we felt that we had heard it all before, we already knew the why and when, and needed to discover only the how.

Over drinks after dinner, Dr Roberts produced a well-thumbed, plastic-covered photo album and proudly related to us how, many years ago, he was the first and only black face to be seen in wig and gown in the official photograph of a dinner of the Inner Temple of London. Pictures of his red Rolls-Royce, his wife and daughter all followed – of which, he hastened to say, he was equally proud. The evening of cognac and storytelling was wrapped up early enough for us to prepare for the next working day.

Sir Alister, with his customary efficiency, had outlined the tasks that each member of the commission was to perform. Mine was to physically inspect the buildings and structures – especially an incomplete hospital being built by a firm of contractors from the People's Republic of China – and to comment on whether their costs were reasonable by Antiguan standards. As a final rejoinder, he warned that our work should be properly documented and supported by evidence (see practice note 38), since, once our investigation was completed, a public hearing on the issue, which in all likelihood would include hostile cross-examination, would be held in St John's.

In the short time that we stayed at the hotel, the group developed a custom of meeting at breakfast to plan the details of the day. I told the group about my Stoppi Basket Index method of costing (as described in my story about Bonaire, and used also in a Pan-American Health Organization investigation into hospital costs in the Bahamas some years before). On this occasion, I said, I would also visit the Public Works Department for basic construction cost information, labour and productivity rates, material costs, extent of local procurement and so on, and to get a general idea of how the local industry worked. This would enable me to work up finished product costs such as square yards of blockwork or tons of reinforcing steel and so on, for use in calculating square footage costs of the various building types under examination. I would then make a trip to the local supermarket to get an idea of the general local cost of living compared to Jamaica and obtain a coefficient for the relative construction costs of the project in question. In this way, based on past experience, I was sure that I would obtain a fairly accurate assessment.

In response to my request, the local director of Public Works invited me to visit. Like many who had begun their career in the civil service under the colonial administration, he was down-to-earth, and in anticipation of my visit, he had the lists of costings that I required ready for me. Over coffee, we talked like old friends, lamenting the decline in quality standards in the building industry that afflicted Antigua as much as Jamaica. He told me how a director of the Medical Benefits Board had dragged him off to China, with little or no briefing, to conclude negotiations for a proposed new hospital with a Chinese construction company of which he had no prior knowledge. He was still seething at the thought that his warning that the awarding of the contract contravened the Antiguan Tender Boards Act was blithely ignored. His sense of public integrity was clearly offended.

In my subsequent interviews with other members of the public service and private sector (contractors, architects and others), I heard similar stories: a government that ran the island with scant regard for the law or the welfare of the inhabitants; girlfriends of cabinet ministers being whisked off in private jets to Miami hospitals, while the ordinary citizens – whose taxes funded the local heath-care system – were unable, in some cases, to obtain even the most basic medical treatment. We were only there to look into the Medical Benefits Scheme, but in the process we soon discovered the extent to which the party in power, and its cronies, were actively and cynically helping to increase the already wide poverty gap.

The MBS scandal, as it became known, was nothing new – it was simply the tip of the iceberg. As in all democracies, there was a small opposition party. Not, on its own, big enough to sway parliament, but strong enough to rally public opinion against the injustices and iniquities being inflicted on the people by their government. Eventually, public opinion and outcry had become too loud for those in power to ignore, and so, with the support of the leaders of the opposition, the governor general issued a proclamation setting up a royal commission of inquiry. A classic example of democracy at work.

Back in Jamaica, our commission completed its work: draft reports, statistics and witness statements were prepared (see practice note 17), debated and eventually compiled into a final report that was submitted to the royal commission prior to the public enquiry. This was later held in Antigua, at a venue appropriately known as the Multi-Purpose Centre, at Perry Bay, St John's. The government was represented by a brilliant barrister from Dominica, one John Astephan, QC, while our team was led by the equally brilliant "Jonny" Cheltenham. As expected, I was cross-examined, but, having been in the "box" in many situations before, I stood up (literally and figuratively) reasonably well. Individuals or small groups of people drifted in and out of the public gallery all the time, but more important, the entire proceedings were televised and covered by the media.

After returning home to Jamaica some time later, I learned that following the exposure and publicity of the findings of the commission of enquiry and its report, excerpts of which were shown on local TV, the ruling party – now with all exposed – had no choice but to call a general election. Unsurprisingly, the opposition won and formed a new government. The bad guys had lost and the good guys had won – but, we pondered, for how long?

8.

Spanish Town

Arbitrators are much like headmasters: they need to maintain an air of authority, to ensure that all the players abide by the rules of the game, keep a semblance of order and discipline at all times and, above all, see that justice is not only done but also seen to be done. A fairly recent case that I presided over as sole arbitrator (beginning in 2004 and ending in 2006) concerned a multiple unit low-income housing development in the suburbs of Spanish Town.

I first visited the historic town in the late 1950s. At the time, it was a sleepy rundown place of about ten to twelve thousand inhabitants, some thirteen miles west of Kingston. Ye Olde Ferry Inn, at Ferry – technically not really part of Spanish Town but close enough to be thought of as such by outsiders – had historically served as a pit-stop where horses could be changed and ladies could refresh themselves when coming to the capital from the country and before entering Kingston, which meant that most Kingstonians thought of the town as a transit point on the main road to the north coast. Spanish Town had a more illustrious past. In the mid-sixteenth century it was the capital of Jamaica, when the Spaniards decided to abandon their initial settlement at Sevilla la Nueva near St Ann's Bay on the north coast (mainly because of the mosquito problem) in favour of the more fertile and pleasant plains farther south. They renamed their new capital St Jago de la Vega. After the English conquest in 1655, it continued to serve as the capital of Jamaica until the Napoleonic Wars, when Britain realized the strategic naval and military significance of Port Royal, and of Kingston, which became the new capital. Since then, Spanish Town had rapidly deteriorated, with only its magnificent Georgian town square heralding its former glory. In the sixties and seventies, the road between Spanish Town and Kingston was considerably improved, which, together with the capital's rapid industrialization and expansion, gave it new life, and it began to serve as a dormitory town of the capital. Local developers were quick to take advantage of the cheap cost of readily available level land so close to Kingston. The rush began in the 1960s and revived again twenty years later, through early developers such as Eddie Lai, H.I. Henriques, the Chang Brothers, and Lucien Chen. Wide-scale construction of affordable housing continued with the introduction of the building societies' input, assistance from the Ministry of Housing, and the creation of the National Housing Trust.

Demand continued unabated until the end of the twentieth century and early 2000s. At this point, the Magil Construction Corporation of Montreal, Canada, entered the picture. An established company that (according to their brochure) had built major structures in Canada and Israel, among other places, they now appeared on the scene as a subcontractor to a well-known local housing developer who had successfully completed other housing projects in Spanish Town. Why? If it was so simple to build mass-housing here, they must have thought, why not be their own developer and reap not just contractor's profit, but all of it? Logical, perhaps, from the developer's point of view, but for us old-timers, the answer to that question was as obvious as a tiger trap in the jungle.

Leaping with both feet, however, they joined up with a local landowner and, with the benevolent support of the housing minister, began in 2002 with the housing development known as Whitewater Meadows. The agreement was, essentially, a partnership between the landowner and Magil as the contractor and implementer of the project, with the ministry acting in the role of "facilitator". Of course, as with all projects of this nature, there were several other colourful characters and sundry hangers-on in the continued saga of the development – opportunists and "margin gatherers", as they are known – but to describe them all, interesting as they may be, would take too much time and certainly expose me to the dangers of the Jamaican laws of libel. Suffice it to say that the developers soon learned that all was not wine and roses in the housing business. The parties clashed over basic interpretations of their contracts, projected sales of units that were meant to help cash-flows did not materialize as planned and, predictably, the more things went pear-shaped, the more the parties fell out.

Eventually, to quote the Jamaican proverb, *Wha' guh bad a mornin' kyahn come good ah evelin'*. The differences and disputes became totally irreconcilable, and, in accordance with the agreement they had signed (see practice note 10), arbitration was called for. Since no arbitrator had been named in advance or agreed upon subsequently, they turned, as prescribed by the contract between them, to the president of the Jamaica Bar Association – then Ms Hilary Phillips, QC – who appointed me to as sole arbitrator in the dispute. My decision would be final and binding on the parties.

The claimant in this case was Magil Construction Jamaica Limited; the respondent was Can-Cara Development Limited.

As I usually do in these matters, to get the ball rolling, I summoned the two parties and their respective legal representatives – both, in this case, well-known firms of Kingston attorneys – for a preliminary meeting, where I spelled out the rules of the game and established the various procedures by which the arbitration would be run, the timetable of the various submissions of one side to the other, the procedures for dealing with witnesses and their swearing in, the records to be kept of the various proceedings, the dates and times of the hearings, the methods by which site visits would be arranged and conducted and so on.

At this point, I normally give participants the opportunity to comment or provide input on these proposed guidelines, but since they are, in the main, procedures developed from past experience, none of them are normally offensive to those involved. On the contrary, attorneys accustomed to traditional law courts usually welcome a firm hand conducting what might otherwise turn into a verbal free-for-all.

The preliminary meeting went reasonably well, the two sides ranged on either side of the conference table, with me at the head. I set dates for the various activities, then sat back and waited. Sure enough, within minutes, the claimant asked that some of their points of claim be changed. As a matter of protocol and courtesy, I put the request to the other side to see if they had any objections. Much to my surprise, they did – complete with pleadings and reasoned arguments. Rather than get into masses of convoluted correspondence to assist me to decide which course to adopt, I told them that I would hold a special hearing to decide on this particular point – the point being not of law, but of procedure.

Acting for the respondent was the illustrious, venerable Jamaican jurist the Honourable Lloyd George Barnett, QC, assisted by attorney Howard Malcolm. Opposing them was a team headed by Mr John Vassel of the Kingston legal firm of Dunn Cox. Although I had, in the past, dealt with some of the leading lights of the Jamaican legal profession, these were the heavyweights indeed.

Acceding to their requests, I received their pleadings (see practice note 15) and then scheduled a meeting for the arguments sometime in June that year. Although I was much struck by the eloquence and erudition of Dr Barnett in particular, after hearing both sides I found in favour of the claimant – namely, that I would allow approved and agreed changes to be made to their pleadings.

As a postscript to this episode, I should point out that I now tell participants in advance – usually at the preliminary meeting – that I will allow agreed amendments to be made, to claims or to the defence, at any time before the beginning of the hearing itself, but obviously not after. In larger and perhaps more important cases, I also require the parties to agree on a "bundle" (see practice note 40) of documents that will be referred to by either side during the hearing(s).

The hearings proper began over a year later, in November 2005. Opening for the claimant, Mr Vassel presented his first witness, someone who was familiar with and had held a position of authority on the site, to provide an overview of the project. He was followed the next day by the presentation of Mr Joseph Gutstadt, president of Magil Construction Limited. A colourful character whose native language was clearly not English, he was of stout build, bald and of medium height, with few other distinguishing characteristics apart from uncontrollable rapid eye movements when stressed.

He was led in evidence on the main issues of their case, but when replying strayed so dramatically and emotionally from the questions put to him as to incur the annoyance not only of the respondent but, it seemed to me, of his own counsel. The day ended, thankfully, without any physical support of the claimant's evidence. I adjourned the hearing until 10 a.m. the following day, with slight trepidation at the thought of the witness's performance under cross-examination.

On resuming proceedings the next morning, I breathed an inward sigh of relief, since everyone present appeared to be in good spirits. Clearly, I said to myself, Mr Vassel had spoken to his witness and briefed him on how to conduct himself for the benefit of his cause. Alas, the good spirits lasted only half an hour or so. Counsel for the respondent – perhaps the most experienced and competent trial lawyer in Jamaica – began very low-key, gradually increasing the complexity of his questions. Time and again, the witness proved unable or unwilling to give a coherent reply, whereupon he would lapse into his emotional mode of gesticulating and raising his voice – no doubt precisely as Dr Barnett had planned.

Feeling that things were getting just a little out of control, I called an early lunch adjournment. On resumption after lunch, we continued with cross-examination, during which Dr Barnett, out of compassion for the witness, I assumed, avoided eliciting emotional responses to his questions, and led him simply to confirm certain contractual and other facts so that they may be entered into the arbitration records.

Here, I should make a point about note-taking and recording of transactions. This is an issue I frequently put to the parties of any dispute. These days, with laptop computers and other electronic devices, things are a lot better, but in the past, with a dearth of court stenographers or computer transcription, I would tell legal counsel of both parties that I recommended someone be appointed to create a transcript of proceedings, provided it was agreed beforehand who footed the bill and that, in any event, I would be given a copy at the end. In the present instance, neither side was willing to incur this cost, and so it was not implemented. This sort of situation places an additional burden on arbitrators, who, like judges, are required to take their own notes of who said what and when, and of everything submitted as evidence. This is more onerous for High and Appeal Court judges, who later, if so requested, are obliged to produce their own transcripts of proceedings.

Over the years, I developed my own personal system of note-taking. I always have three pens in front of me – green, red and black. With my own form of shorthand, I record everything the claimant says in green, the respondent's statements in red, and all my instructions and comments (including impressions about either of the parties or witnesses) in black. Over the years I have found this system most effective. This was especially so in one case where the attorney for the losing party vociferously and demonstrably insisted that I immediately provide him with a copy of my transcript. In keeping with my pacifist tradition, I eventually provided the document to him. This was immediately followed by a further vigorous demand for an immediate interpretation of my notes. No prize for guessing my response!

To return to the hearing: Mr Gutstadt had reached the end of his cross-examination and was now being re-examined by Mr Vassel. Relieved, perhaps, at being freed from the pressure cooker of Dr Barnett's close scrutiny, he now appeared to lose all restraint and, in a bid to drive home what he perceived to be the validity of his case, even used the occasion to bypass his attorney and shout at me, at times emotionally and in languages unfamiliar to most of us in the room. Happily, I was able to keep the peace until adjournment, although I admit I came perilously close to either shutting down the proceedings or, even worse, joining in the fray myself. In a bid to introduce into proceedings a measure of calm and clarity (see practice note 8), it occurred to me that now would be a good time to arrange a site meeting, although this had not been scheduled in the original timetable. I ordered this to take place the next day and, resisting offers from both sides of transport to Spanish Town in order to maintain my impartiality, opted to drive there independently.

At the site meeting the next day, I was shown the houses and their infrastructure, the parts of the scheme pertaining to the dispute, the proximity to sewage and water services, and so on. Throughout the visit, both sides were exceedingly polite, to each other and to me, perhaps because the claimant, feeling comfortable on home turf, was happily jumping in and out of culverts and pointing out items of his interest. Once the site visit was concluded, I informed everyone present that we would resume the remainder of the hearings the next day, at the usual venue, then I bid them all goodbye and returned to town, my fingers crossed.

The following morning at the appointed time, I called the hearing to order, but the main witness, Mr Gutstadt, was nowhere to be found (see practice note 16). I usually allow participants twenty minutes grace at the start of my hearings in case of unforeseen issues such as heavy traffic.

Half an hour went by.

Experience has taught me to expect anything in arbitrations, including the non-appearance of participants (see practice notes 33 and 34). In such instances – where one side is present or represented and the other is absent – an arbitrator can proceed by issuing what is known as an *ex parte* order (see practice note 28). This allows him to proceed with the hearings with only one party present. It need only be issued once by the arbitrator to be valid throughout the dispute hearings, and for that reason, to be on the safe side, I usually do this at the time of the preliminary meeting, just in case.

I informed the meeting that in the absence of the main witness, I intended to proceed, but that in the interests of parity and equality, I would be especially vigilant in maintaining impartiality during the remainder of evidence. The rest of the hearing proceeded normally, and after requesting final written submissions to be delivered to me within a specified time, I closed the hearings. Still no sign of our mysterious friend, Mr Gutstadt.

Days and weeks went by while I patiently waited to finalize this matter. Eventually I duly received the final written submissions of both parties and spent considerable time assessing the various arguments and merits of each one. At the end of my deliberations, I reached my decision, which was, as you may have gathered by now, in favour of the respondent, with costs (including my fees) to be borne by the claimant. This was in keeping with the principle of awarding costs to "follow the event" – that is, the arbitrator decides, after ensuring that the application for costs is both allowable and reasonable and, based on his award, usually states that the loser pays the costs, apportioned as the arbitrator sees appropriate (see practice note 42). Here, I was faced with a dilemma. This occurs when an arbitrator's fees and expenses have been assessed to the losing party, and that party, with the certain knowledge that they have lost, may simply walk away from the arbitration. This leaves the poor arbitrator to face the only remedy available: the court. In this case, I had only myself to blame. I had failed to exercise the arbitrator's legal right to withhold the award if it includes their fees and costs, until duly collected by both parties and paid for. My award was in favour of the claimant, and by withholding the award until I was paid by the respondent, I was actually penalizing the claimant. The principle at stake then was not actually legal, but rather moral or ethical. After due consideration, I decided that my conscience was of greater importance than my bank balance and so released my award to both parties simultaneously.

I later learned from the claimant that the respondent, Mr Gutstadt, probably anticipating my decision and having gotten himself into further problems – as I later learned he had with others in relation to this and other housing scheme operations in Jamaica – had quietly skipped the country before the end of the hearing, never to return.

Commentary

One of the advantages in favour of arbitration over litigation is that arbitration is private, and no publicity or release of information concerning the arbitration is allowed except with the consent of the parties or an order of the arbitrator. This is opposite the public nature of litigation, where the media is allowed access to cases and their subsequent right of publication.

So it was, totally without my knowledge or consent, or as far as I was aware those of the parties, that an article appeared in the Jamaica *Daily Observer* in 13 May 2006:

> Housing Developer Leaves Jamaica with Bitter Taste
> Magil Construction Limited, the Canadian-based development company that began constructing houses here in 1997, has pulled out of Jamaica citing wanton corruption from government officers, parish council members and community extortion that has costed them in excess of $130 million.
> After completing the 468 unit Magil Palms, its latest housing project, Magil President Jose [*sic*] Gutstadt said his company decided to discontinue any further operations in Jamaica indefinitely.

Continuing later in the article it was further reported that, "in the meantime, the Jamaica Mortgage Bank (JMB) on Thursday refuted claims that it has placed Magil in receivership, saying instead that the company has failed to satisfy the repayment agreement on the Magil Palms Housing Development" and concluded in the same vein, without any reference to our arbitration which had begun as early as 2002.

The matter was later picked up by the Jamaica *Gleaner* in their issue of 18 July 2006 with the banner headline "Developers Win $165m Award Against Magil". Their report was less dramatic than the *Observer* and began as follows:

> After four years of arbitration, Can-Cara Developments Limited, developers of the White Water Housing Scheme in St Catherine, has been awarded more than $165 million against co-developers Magil Construction Jamaica Limited.
>
> The award is the outcome of an arbitration matter which began in April 2002 and was settled earlier this month, over the dispute in a co-development agreement between both parties.

The report further stated: "However, the Can-Cara officials revealed that the manhunt is on for Mr Gutstadt. We can pursue Magil in any part of the world to recover this money and we intend to do that."

Fortunately neither the name of the arbitrator nor of anyone on the legal team that participated in this arbitration was mentioned in any reporting I saw at the time.

What this example does point out, however, is the care arbitrators must take to ensure that nothing they do or say while they are in control of the arbitral proceedings can be used by any disgruntled party.

9.

Grand Cayman

My first trip to the Cayman Islands was in the late 1960s, at the invitation of a Caymanian attorney, who was resident in Cayman and familiar with the area but less so with the intricacies of alternative dispute resolution. I was invited there to advise and guide him on an alternative method of settling his involvement in a building dispute – arbitration perhaps, although not necessarily – arising from his involvement as the developer of the construction of a three-storey office building, one of the first such modern multi-storey structures to be built on the island.

The journey from Jamaica began with a hair-raising flight in a small six-seater propeller aircraft of unknown vintage, at a low altitude due to the lack of pressurization and other flight conveniences that we now take for granted. After landing on what might charitably be called a converted country road (although what it was before conversion is anyone's guess) in a desolate area we were told was the "Owen Roberts Airfield", a motley crew of laconic, overall-clad ground staff sauntered over to the now-stationary craft and placed next to the exit a little wooden flight of steps – which, as one self-appointed wit on the plane remarked, was almost as rickety as the aircraft itself. Once on the safety of the ground, we all breathed a sigh of relief, several passengers quietly genuflecting.

Alas, we relaxed too soon. Before arriving, we had all heard of tales of the legendary Cayman mosquitos, their size, aggression and tenacity; locals dismissed these allegations with a kiss of the teeth and flamboyant hand gestures. Yet we were forcibly reminded of those stories as soon as we disembarked. Without warning, we were subjected to a relentless and merciless attack by what I could only describe as Cayman kamikaze stingers.

They were every bit as bad as we had been warned and then some, giving no quarter, zooming in perfect formations at any exposed section of skin. The ground staff, little wooden steps in hand, ushered us as quickly as possible into the comparative safety of the customs shed. Lest I be taken to task by the Cayman Islands Department of Tourism, I hasten to add that in the intervening years, the breeding grounds of their mosquitoes, the swamps, have been drained, the infrastructure improved and the mosquito infestation more or less eradicated.

Another tidbit worth noting, for those unfamiliar with this part of the world, is that prior to Jamaican independence in 1962, the Cayman Islands were colonial dependencies of Jamaica. Initially dubbed *Las Tortugas* by Columbus when he first sighted them in 1503, by dint of the many turtles found there, the three islands – Grand Cayman (76 square miles), Cayman Brac (15 square miles) and Little Cayman (11 square miles) – which lie approximately 430 miles south of Miami, were ceded to the British by Spain in the Treaty of Madrid of 1670. It is also amusing to relate that in spite of most immediate postwar colonial territories struggling and in some cases fighting their colonial power for independence, Grand Cayman, to this day, steadfastly insists on remaining a British colonial territory.

Long before there was a tourist industry, these small, somewhat isolated islands were a refuge for itinerant fishermen, pirates and privateers. The local populace, small and introspective (evident even today in the predominance of certain surnames), settled and developed whatever opportunities their agriculture or geography encouraged. Thus, while the larger islands such as Jamaica and Cuba developed their agriculture (sugar cane, bananas and so on) for export to the mother country, then considered to be England, others, particularly in the days of US prohibition, took advantage of their proximity to the United States and exhibited resourcefulness of another kind: smuggling from the rum-producing islands to both the United States and Canada. Cuba, then under the control of the US branch of the mafia, had their own system and organization for exporting rum to the United States; from other sources of origin, Cayman was then an ideal trans-shipment point for entry through the porous southern US border. In addition, the founding fathers of the Cayman Islands had the business acumen and foresight to declare their island tax- and duty-free. Since then, apart from their great success at subsequently developing a highly efficient and attractive tourist industry, the Caymans' tax haven has contributed greatly to the economic success and later development of the country.

All this interesting and educational stuff I learned from my taxi driver Harold, who was to take me in his, even then, rather ancient Morris Oxford to one of the few organized public hotels on the island. I've long since forgotten its name; it consisted of widely spaced, timber-framed and mosquito-screened single-storey cottages located on what would later become the famous Seven Mile Beach. His final instruction to me was, "I'll drop you, Sar, as close as I can to your cottage – den run fas to Reception to try to avoid the mossies 'dem – after dat, run back unto the screenin', fast like." His good advice was well taken.

The rest of the story of my first visit is uneventful. The issues, as I said, were comparatively simple. The parties to the dispute – my client the employer, his designer and a local contractor – were all more than courteous. The meetings and discussions were conducted in one of the empty cottages on the beach. I began by explaining my role in the matter, and how, in a more formal setting, this initial phase of the proceedings would be called a preliminary meeting; how I would prefer to receive evidence (see practice note 38) and pleadings; and that my role in this matter was one of strict impartiality. This was put to the test at the end of the first day's session, when I was invited to drinks and dinner by both parties. I explained, as diplomatically as possible, that I would be delighted to have dinner with all of them together, or, regrettably, neither. Needless to say, for the remainder of proceedings, I dined alone. Looking back, I was perhaps a little too fastidious on insisting this, but I was much younger and less experienced then and still believed in the rigidity and discipline of rules of professional conduct.

The first full day was devoted to the introductory meeting, in which I explained to the parties what I call "The Rules of the Game". I have always found that a little time spent on this aspect at the outset can save time – and avoid much confusion – later. Both sides were represented by counsel who, I was happy to note, agreed to most of my suggestions. (I later heard from both that this was a learning experience they appreciated.) A site visit with all relevant parties present was high on my agenda.

The participants in this case were, as is often the case, the employer (client) and the contractor. Both were Caymanian: the client, a member of a well-known and old established legal family, and the contractor, a recent entrant in the industry. Both sides pleaded their respective viewpoints with such advantages that they had the employer stressing his social and economic status, and the contractor his emotive skills. There was little actual law in the arguments of either side, which involved mainly traditional claims and counterclaims of failure to keep to schedule, underpayment, cost of changes, time extensions and so on. Sensing the largely technical nature of the dispute, the attorneys of the two sides contributed little to the site visit, and I listened politely to everything said or shown to me without comment or response, knowing from experience that the parties must feel that they have had the equivalent of their "day in court" and the opportunity to get all their points across as convincingly as possible.

As always in arbitration, after listening to all the pleadings and arguments, I made my decision based on all the facts presented in whatever form, mixing in my own personal ingredients of experience, technical knowledge of the issues involved and, above all, a large portion of natural justice.

The arbitration lasted four days, during which all the usual formalities and sequence of activities were diplomatically arranged by me. Between sessions and in the early morning (the best time to observe the large and varied non-aggressive stingrays), I made the most of the sand, sea and sun. (In the process, I learned a very important thing about mosquitoes: they do not like the sea and stay away from it. Which meant that the more time I spent in the ocean, the less chance I had of being bitten – which suited me just fine.) I encouraged closing addresses, then thanked all who had contributed to the exercise for their patience and hospitality and closed the hearing (see practice note 22).

My departure, assisted by my friend Harold, mirrored my arrival: same rickety wooden steps, same airfield mosquito contingent, same scary aircraft.

Back in my office in Kingston, I was able to consider the evidence I had received and my impressions of the parties and witnesses, and, after a week or so (and receipt of the final portion of my fee), I transmitted my award simultaneously to the parties' attorneys in Grand Cayman. I learned later that it was received and accepted without adverse comment from either parties. I looked forward to further encounters on this delightful small island.

Sometime later, another invitation arrived, this time from another firm of Caymanian attorneys, large and prestigious, whose offices were housed in one of the new multi-storey air-conditioned office buildings in George Town. It was one of several to have been developed in response to the rapid expansion of the successful tourist and commercial development that had taken place since last I was there.

What a difference a decade made. This time, transportation to the island was by a scheduled jetliner, which landed at what was now officially the Owen Roberts International Airport, and which now routinely accommodated jumbo aircraft. We disembarked by means of proper mobile stairs, and there was, I was happy to note, no delegation of kamikaze mosquitoes to greet us on our short walk into a new air-conditioned terminal. Customs and immigration procedures were handled with courtesy and in total comfort. Exiting, I enquired after my old taxi friend Harold, but he must have passed on years ago, as no one had heard of him. Instead, I was whisked away in a new vehicle to a new hotel, which this time was not at the seafront. There was far too much construction activity taking place on Seven Mile Beach, and, in any event, the few new luxury hotels or condominiums that had been constructed were not only high-priced but fully occupied. Clearly, I thought to myself, the island's prosperity was a different order of magnitude compared to what I'd observed on my previous visit. Instead, I was taken to a hotel across the street from the beach, one that had been there for some time and, predictably, was slated for demolition and reconstruction as a multi-storey resort chain hotel.

Boosted by the island's growing reputation as an international tax haven, George Town had, in the years since my previous visit, expanded to the point where it now reached, and surrounded, the airport. Most of this development was of commercial offices for international as well as local banks, firms of attorneys and accountants, and myriad services supporting that industry.

One of these new multi-storey office buildings was the reason for my invitation. The owner, a local entrepreneur, had decided that what was needed was a particular kind of building, with integrated parking. When construction began, however, this proved to be rather impractical, from a structural point of view apart from anything else. In the preliminary correspondence and briefings I had received in Kingston from the attorneys representing the two sides, I believed the situation was obvious: the consultants – architects, structural and mechanical engineers, quantity surveyors and so on – had been intimidated by the client's status and possible local influence, to the extent that they had refrained from advising him that the building simply would not work the way he had asked them to design it. As a result, tenders had been issued in the normal way, contractors appointed and work had commenced on-site before the problem became apparent. It was all as clear as crystal, I thought to myself, and with this preconceived position already formed in my mind – a condition I perpetually warn others to avoid in preference to the principle of always keeping an open mind on issues until all facts area known – I departed for Cayman.

Reflecting on that point prior to my arrival in Cayman, I recalled that to pre-judge an issue was a common trap so easy for arbitrators to fall into. I remembered how often in the past I had formed opinions on the relative rights and wrongs of the parties in a dispute, only to be embarrassed later, on receiving valid evidence, perhaps previously undisclosed, that forced me to revise my conclusions (see practice note 2). The lesson I had learned from those experiences I had never forgotten: always keep an open mind during the evidence and arguments stage of proceedings; make copious notes of important issues or statements for future reference; take note of people's body language and attitudes (which reveal a great deal about deceit and honesty); and above all, wait until all the dust of judicial conflict has settled before even attempting to arrive at any decisions. Even then, sleep on it for at least two days before issuing the final award.

In George Town, counsel for one side produced documents and evidence of the other's professional negligence, which were countered by accusations of contractual irresponsibility by not identifying impracticalities prior to construction and so on. In terms of the actual building, by mutual agreement progress had been halted pending the outcome of these hearings. Foundations had been completed, but the construction of the superstructure depended almost entirely on how the two intended functions of offices and parking could be reconciled without compromising the infrastructure of the electrical and mechanical services already in place.

Both sides pleaded their respective cases with great competence. I duly observed, listened, read and absorbed all the evidence presented. I had expected to reach some sort of conclusion before returning to Kingston, but in truth, at the closing of the hearing I was in a complete quandary: both sides had perfectly good arguments – one for designing the building the way they had, and the other for objecting to the design because it was impractical. Alone in my hotel room, I agonized, turning the coin of natural justice over and over again in my mind, but no solution presented itself. I had no choice but to dine alone and sleep on it, in the hope that some breakthrough would occur to me overnight.

The next morning was magnificent: a clear blue sky, a slight cooling breeze from the north and an early morning sun lighting up the eastern sky. How perfect, I thought to myself, before remembering my still unsolved dilemma. Then suddenly – out of the blue, as it were – the solution occurred to me with startling clarity. After a hurried breakfast, I phoned the two parties for one last meeting before my departure.

They arrived, somewhat puzzled, having been under the impression that I had concluded the hearings. I asked the attorneys representing the parties if they would allow me to suggest a change in the programme. I explained that I had found the evidence of both sides equally convincing and therefore thought that an arbitral decision was not the best solution to their rather thorny problem. I further suggested that a departure from my terms of reference would need to be agreed on by the parties.

"It seems to me," I said, "that both parties still harbour a certain amount of goodwill towards each other, and wish to continue their future contractual relationship as well as to pursue the project to completion. I also recognize that there may have been, prior to contract, certain design misunderstandings on the part of the architects and engineers, and the absence of a legal stipulation for the contractor not to proceed with construction on realizing that the design was impractical and, finally, a certain innocence on the part of the owner after the signing of the construction contract."

Pausing to allow these basic emotional, though not entirely contractual, facts to sink in, I continued: "It seems to me, then, that arbitration, in the strict meaning of the term, is *not* what is required in these circumstances. The typical terms of my arbitrator's reference are to issue an enforceable award at the end of these proceedings. I can do this, of course, but I fear that it would be neither judicially constructive nor what the parties want. Instead, I would like, with your joint permission, to propose a viable alternative."

The attorneys were all ears at this point.

"On our joint site inspection three days ago, I observed the contract work in progress, as well as the impasse that continuing those works would entail. I further pondered on what kind of technical, financial or contractual solution would be equitable for me to hand down to the parties. After much soul-searching and deliberation, I realized that neither party would benefit from any of the traditional penal solutions. What I did observe, however, at our site meeting, was an empty lot adjoining the site in question.

"If you remember, gentlemen, I enquired as to the ownership of that adjacent plot, and was told that it belonged to the claimant in this dispute. My proposal, therefore, is for the employer (claimant) to arrange that this land be transferred, at an agreed valuation, to the contractor carrying out this construction, and for the technical/ professional consultants to redesign the project so that this adjoining site is used as a multi-storied carpark, and connect it to the office building on the existing site, so as to make the entire scheme workable."

I paused to see their reaction. I was taking a bit of a gamble: they could either embrace the new compromise scheme, or advise me that my services were no longer required. I had decided that the risk was worth it, for the sake of natural justice.

As expected, the attorneys asked for an hour's adjournment to consult their principals, which I granted. After only half an hour, they reentered the arbitration room and announced that, after a brief discussion, both parties had agreed to the idea. They asked if upon my return to Jamaica, I would be so kind as to draw up a draft of a consent award (see practice note 36) to that effect – with, they added, my assessment of the necessary extensions of time and professional fees that would be required; what changes (if any) would need to be made in the terms and conditions of the existing building contract; and last, if they were to consider any fiscal penalties or benefits accruing to each of the parties as a result of this new agreement.

I was, I must confess, immensely relieved that my plan had worked, and that the principle of arbitration had been preserved.

I duly returned to Kingston and drafted a consent award, which I transmitted to the parties' attorneys and which was, after a short time, returned, ratified by both parties, and finally published. It had ended, I was happy to note, with a win-win situation. It could so easily have gone the other way.

Over the years, the centre of the capital, George Town, had grown haphazardly at the whim and fancy of its merchants. Now, in the early twenty-first century, the government decided to consolidate all its offices, which had previously been scattered around the town centre, into a single modern administrative complex. Rather than employing a plethora of professional consultants, as the present system demanded, a "design-and-build" contract was chosen as the best and most cost-effective and efficient method of getting this building completed. To this end, both parties – namely, the government and the appointed design/builder – chose to base their agreement on the American Institute of Architects standard design-and-build contract. This states that the designer/builder is responsible for all design matters – from identification of all the client's needs, through design and costing of all electrical and mechanical services, to a provisional final budget figure of the completed project. This figure is then negotiated between the client's representative and the design/build contractor to reach a final binding cost. Once all the details of the new project are ironed out, a written contract setting out all the rights and obligations of both parties is signed, a mobilization payment issued, and the project begins.

This particular system has many advantages over the traditional method of construction, which requires one to find and choose the "right" architect; to tackle the complexities of understanding and specifying the appropriate electrical and mechanical services for the building, and – under the British system – employing additional professional consultants, such as quantity surveyors, to list and cost all construction components; and spend yet more time negotiating individual prices or rates. The advantages, of course, are evident. The simplicity of dealing directly with a single entity – the designer-builder – means that specifications and costs are more easily negotiated and established, and the design developed in partnership. Conversely, perhaps as a benefit over the traditional method of acquisition of buildings, the system also imposes a strict discipline on the part of the employer to ensure that all matters concerning design and contractual conditions are predetermined and included in the final contract document.

In other words, unlike in the traditional system, the entire responsibility for proper execution of the contract is placed upon the designer-builder (usually the contractor), down to the smallest detail in the set of contract drawings and specifications, which form the core of the contract between owner and contractor. As a result, the designer-builder is motivated and indeed in some cases entitled to claim for additional costs and time from the employer (client) in response to variations to the work under construction in the execution of the original contract.

Such was the case in the proposed construction of a new central administrative building for the Cayman Islands with design-build contractors McAlpine Limited, a reputable and experienced contractor that had built several of the new and impressive commercial and resort buildings on the island, and the government's chief architect.

The contract that the parties had entered into was based on the American Institute of Architects standard design-and-build contract, adapted for use in Grand Cayman. It contained all the usual clauses, including those dealing with dispute resolution, specifically article 10: "The parties are fully committed to working with each other throughout the project and to communicate regularly with each other at all times, so as to avoid and resolve claims, disputes or controversies . . . if not, then the parties shall submit the dispute to non-binding mediation. . . . The mediation shall be conducted pursuant to a mediation agreement negotiated by the parties."

It transpired that there were, in fact, several points of disagreement that evolved subsequent to the commencement of this contract. Under the above terms, and after both parties had agreed to my nomination, I was duly appointed and named in the contract as the mediator referred to in article 10. I asked if there was a standard set of Cayman Islands rules on mediation that governed such disputes, but both parties pleaded ignorance and suggested that I provide my own. Since at that time (mid-2007) I was in the process of drawing up a set of standard rules for arbitration, mediation and adjudication for use in Jamaica, it was a simple matter for me to construct a set for Cayman – which happily met with no opposition from either party.

All proceeded swimmingly until, one day in January 2009, a letter arrived from the Cayman government's chief project manager advising me, in accordance with the aforementioned article 10, of the items of dispute that the parties wished to bring to mediation. Under the very rules that I had drafted earlier, as mediator, I had fifteen days to respond and a further fifteen days to present a "settlement document" to a joint meeting of the parties, announcing the results of the mediation process with respect of all the disputed issues, for them to ratify and return.

Fortunately, my schedule allowed me the luxury of choosing a mutually acceptable date, well within the stipulated time limit, to get across and begin the process. As on the previous occasion, I was impressed by the continuing improvements to the airport terminal in the years since my previous visit and the general upgrading of all the island's infrastructure. The sleepy, laid-back Caribbean island that I had first encountered in the 1960s had been transformed, as if by a magic wand, into a Florida-style resort – to the dismay, perhaps, of some traditionalists. I was further gratified at being whisked, in true VIP style, out of the immigration queue and into a waiting government vehicle.

Wasting no time, after checking in at the hotel I began my assignment, as always, by summoning the parties of the dispute to a preliminary meeting to establish the rules of the game, and in particular to explain how this mediation process would differ from the more familiar process of arbitration.

First I always assure the parties that I have no bias or preferences in this matter, and that my only objective is to act as "enabler" – one who understands the issues, and only expresses an opinion when asked to do so by both parties – so that each party may appreciate the other's position, and emotion is replaced by logic (or, failing that, by the agreed contract conditions). I also emphasized that neither party should expect as a matter of course to receive 100 per cent of their claim, and indeed that each must enter the mediation process prepared to relinquish at least part of their claim in exchange for an equitable settlement. To help them in this regard, I also reminded them to bear in mind the considerable extra cost of formal arbitration proceedings, should the mediation process fail. I also emphasized that, under the terms of the contract or rules, I had no authority to impose a settlement upon the parties; however, with goodwill on both sides, considerable progress may be made, and a reasonable settlement may be reached. Finally, I assured all present that all discussions and material generated by our proceedings would be treated as confidential, and not subject to disclosure in any subsequent proceedings – unless I was ordered to do so by a court of law. Neither party had any questions or comments.

We reconvened the next day in the client's conference room to discuss strategy. In accordance with standard mediation practice, my plan was to meet separately with each of the parties – first with the claimant (the designer-builder), then with the respondent (government representatives), followed by successive alternating meetings of this sort, culminating in a joint meeting, on day three or four, perhaps, to review and finalize the results of the mediation process. In the interim, at my request, there would also be a joint inspection of the site and of the work completed to date, for me to get a feel for the items in dispute. At least, that was the plan.

Alas, my appeals at the preliminary meeting to each side to embrace such lofty ideals as mutual understanding and co-operation and to adopt a "give-and-take" attitude in reaching a reasonable settlement were utterly ignored. It quickly became apparent that those responsible for the negotiations prior to mediation had not espoused the charitable attitudes and generosity of spirit required for a successful mediation, and consequently both sides had come to the table with entrenched positions and attitudes and were intent on arguing their respective cases as though in a courtroom. The representatives of both sides, it seemed, felt bolstered by the authority of their status in their respective organizations to stick to a "take no prisoners" attitude.

Unfortunately, no amount of "shuttle diplomacy" on my part – including reminders to both sides of the high cost and protracted nature of arbitration that would become inevitable if the issue were not resolved this way – was enough to persuade the two sides to drop their uncompromising stances. I was disappointed, but I was (and, I hope, remain) a realist, so when the regrettable and hollow sound after the third unsuccessful day was that of the other shoe dropping and, I reminded myself in some measure of consolation that, in mediation as in real life, one can lead a horse to water, but one cannot make him drink.

Later that day and prior to my departure, I ruminated on the failure of my mission. I reviewed my strategy and attempts at mediating what otherwise might have been simple, albeit compromise, solutions to the conflict. On reflection, I became convinced that there really was, irrespective of the wording of their own contractual obligations, no great willingness to compromise or even to arrive at a mutually equitable solution to their issues. A mediation is not a negotiation, nor is it a legal conflict; we exist not to impose solutions but to facilitate and assist the parties in arriving at their own settlements. If they eventually elect not to keep to those basic rules, consensus being of paramount importance, then they are free to go their separate ways.

On departing, I mentioned to one of the parties who had kindly offered me a lift to the airport that "perhaps the passage of time after this salutary experience may have the effect of softening both positions and engender a willingness to try the process again".

"Don't hold your breath, Stoppi," came the pessimistic reply.

10.

Hill People

One finds, in the Caribbean, an interesting pattern in demographic settlement over time. In the countries originally settled by the Spanish – for example, Colombia and Venezuela – the capital cities were usually situated at the approximate geographic centre of the country, and at the highest elevation that was practical for the settlers. Conversely, the countries discovered or conquered by the British had their capital cities sited adjoining harbours or defensible bases for their naval fleets.

This early pattern was reflected over the next few centuries in the expansion of those cities. The ruling and wealthy classes of English settlements prefer to remain close to their commercial ventures downtown and in close proximity to the wharves and warehouses of merchant importers and exporters, while the lower economic levels of society – later to burgeon rapidly, assisted by the abolition of slavery – sought the higher elevations adjoining the city for their expansion. As with the well-documented example of the favelas of Rio de Janeiro, Kingston and its surrounding area – commonly known in Jamaica as the parish of St Andrew – and most of the English-speaking capitals of the Caribbean are good examples of this phenomenon. Indeed, in Jamaica the marginalization of the poor – both metaphorically and physically – has led to the expansion not just of poor neighbourhoods on the outskirts of Kingston, but also a proliferation of villages and small townships well beyond the parish boundaries, almost to the foothills of the Blue Mountains themselves.

Idyllic though some of the latter locations may be, accessibility is a problem, one made worse by the lack of proper road maintenance, which leads to serious problems after almost every hurricane or rainy season.

To deal with these issues – since most of these areas fall outside the jurisdiction of any parish council – the Jamaican government established the
Jamaica Social Investment Fund. This functions much like a development
bank, dispensing grants for small, localized social projects and funding
and implementing projects that would normally be too modest to qualify
for inclusion in the main government agency programmes for the building
or repair contracts involved in these projects and the selection of contractors. The documentation is simple enough not to require the involvement
of outside lawyers and professionals, and instead is developed in-house by
staff of the Jamaica Social Investment Fund.

Usually, the beneficiaries of such mini-projects are local social groups, or
local contractors using local labour, which in itself is a boost for the community in question. In recognition of the need for some provision for conflict
resolution, a simple arbitration clause was inserted into these contracts.
The procedures set out therein are similar to what emerged later, in more
sophisticated forms, in the area of adjudication. Simply put, an arbitrator
is named in the agreement, and that individual is made available on call to
inspect, meet the parties and hand down a decision, without unnecessarily
protracted hearings, legalities, exchanges of reams of evidence and so on.

Over the years, I have been called upon to attend on a few of these cases.
I always looked forward to an enjoyable trip to the cool and extraordinary
beauty of the mountains, especially in the height of summer. I appreciated
the leisurely drive through the small villages, stopping now and then to chat
with someone on the roadside, and, eventually, after negotiating one or two
hair-raising mountain roads, arriving at the site – the *locus quo* – where
the participants would be waiting for their day in court.

The first example to relate, typical in scope and character, was where
a short section of retaining wall made of rubble stone had been washed
away by a recent flash flood. The footings were still intact, but about forty
feet of wall, complete with belt course and capping, had disappeared down
the mountain slope. The contract documents spoke only of replacing the
missing section. The contractor claimed for extra costs, since a smaller
and subsequent downpour had prevented his pouring of the concrete belt
course; the Jamaica Social Investment Fund inspector disputed this, an
impasse was reached and work had stopped. I was called in to adjudicate.

I asked the builder (the claimant in this instance) to state his case, which he did amid much theatrical waving of arms, to indicate the enormous flood that had kept his workers from completing the casting. At regular intervals, the workmen (and the occasional workwoman) chimed in, as in a Greek chorus, vociferously confirming the veracity of their boss's claim. By this time, in true Jamaican fashion, a small group of other locals had gathered to add their unsolicited evidence to that of the contractor and his gang of fervent supporters. In the spirit of natural justice (and, I admit, also because I was secretly enjoying this seemingly choreographed display of country drama), I asked the contractor if he had anything else to tell me. Looking slightly abashed and waiting for some prompting from the audience (which never came) he looked down and said, "No."

I invited the inspector to give his version of events, and his reaction to the contractor's claim. Speaking much more matter-of-factly than the contractor, and bereft of the vocal and moral support of the onlookers, he spoke of the excessiveness of the claim, and the need for the contractor to assume most, if not all, the risk of water disturbing his work, especially since we were now well into the rainy season. Thus concluded the presentation of evidence.

In Jamaica, no self-respecting builder concludes a site meeting without lunch. Accordingly, at this moment, two prettily dressed women with matching head-ties, who had been unobserved during the presentation of evidence, began a charcoal fire upon which were placed several kerosene oil pans. Sensing my cue, and in accordance with local custom, I offered my brief concluding remarks, in which I thanked the participants for the clarity and comprehensiveness of their evidence and told them that my award would be delivered to them by the end of the week.

The ladies then emerged, bearing plates of steaming boiled banana, dumplings, duckanoo wrapped in banana leaf, and, of course, the ubiquitous Jamaican dish of rice and peas, which we all consumed with gusto. I then delivered my closing speech, as expected by protocol, in which I politely thanked the contractor, his Greek chorus, the inspector, and the ladies who provided the delicious lunch.

By week's end, as promised, I had written what I considered a fair award and sent it off to the parties. Since I subsequently received no threatening letters or other signs of protest, I assume my decision was accepted.

On another occasion, similarly in the hill country, another dispute arose –
this time of a political nature. In Jamaica, as in other parts of the developing world, given high unemployment and few opportunities to earn a
decent wage, the employment of labour on a construction site, skilled and
unskilled, is not simply a matter of obtaining the right number of workers
to do the job, but also of providing an economic boost to areas normally
starved of such opportunities. The selection of workers is hugely critical to
the lives of residents in the area of the construction project, since employment income represents the difference between abject poverty and a marginal existence. Consequently, in some areas, particularly during times
of economic downturn, competition for construction jobs has resulted in
violence and riots. In Jamaica, the unions responsible for regulating and
contracting labour are invariably affiliated with one political party or
another, so employment selections are a highly political issue.

As in many countries, each of the two main political parties – the left-
wing People's National Party (PNP) and the Jamaica Labour Party (JLP,
which, despite its name, is socially conservative) – is associated with a certain colour: orange for the PNP and green for the JLP. At the time of this
tale, a by-election was about to be held in a particular constituency in the
parish of St Mary.

After driving up to the site in question, I immediately spotted the reason
for the dispute, which had nothing to do with contract law or the quality
of the work. The incumbent local member of Parliament, who had recently
passed away, was a member of the ruling JLP party, which had held a slim
majority in the last general election. The opposition was now confident of
unseating the incumbent party and winning the by-election – so much so,
in fact, that the contractor (who evidently was a JLP supporter) had felt
compelled to provide most of the labourers on-site with green shirts, in the
hope of turning the tide in favour of the JLP after all. The local opposition
(PNP) candidate, clearly up in arms about this, was loudly demanding
that his supporters among the labourers be allowed to wear orange shirts.

Taking a deep breath, I emerged from my car and signalled the representatives of both sides – including the contractor and the neutral employer's
supervisor – to an on-site conference. I began my usual introductory speech
on virtues of unity and peace in the cause of national development and

progress (about which, when I'm in the mood, I can be quite persuasive), and was so engrossed in it that I failed to notice lunchtime had arrived, and – right on cue – proceedings were interrupted by copious quantities of cooked food that miraculously appeared. The meal was shared, in an atmosphere of great conviviality, among green and orange shirts alike, and, of course, myself.

Since there was little else to do by way of evidence, I concluded proceedings immediately after lunch and promised delivery of an award within forty-eight hours. After sleeping on the matter, I issued my award the following day, in which I ordered that, in keeping with the human right of personal expression, operatives on site should be permitted to wear the shirt colour of their choice, and that any attempt to prevent this would be considered contempt of court. (This was patently untrue, of course – but neither party knew this.)

Nothing more was heard on the matter. Both sides were satisfied with the opportunity to have had their say, and they accepted the decision.

Sometime in late 2013, I received another enquiry from the same government organization to deal with a minor dispute concerning the construction of a simple basketball court at the Lluidas Vale "sports complex". The work consisted of clearing the overgrown bush covering the small site and its resurfacing which originally had been incorrectly laid. The contract sum was not significant, and the completion time for the work was twenty-eight days. Totally uncomplicated. (Ha!)

My main reason for including this tale is the historic interest of the region and its location of natural beauty deep in the Juan de Bolas mountains in the parish of Clarendon. One approaches Lliudas Vale from Kingston by branching west off the main road at Moneague and climbing gradually through winding, narrow country roads until reaching the crest, which overlooks the fertile sugar-cane lands of the valley below. This is the estate known as Worthy Park. Long before it earned that name, the area was settled by a Spanish slave named Juan de Bolas, who had been allowed by his conquistador owners to raise cattle. After the English capture of the island in 1655, he led a group of similarly freed slaves, headed by General Ysassi, to assist the remaining Spanish resistance to the English occupation.

When eventually discovered several years later, de Bolas changed sides in exchange for the grant of citizenship, and formed one of the first free black settlements in the New World.

Following his role in the capture of Jamaica, Oliver Cromwell in 1670 rewarded one of his generals, Francis Pike, for his part in that success with a land patent to more than three hundred acres of prime farm land – which over the years expanded to almost five thousand acres. This estate, later known as Worthy Park, devolved at the beginning of the twentieth century to a Jamaican family, who continue to produce sugar there.

Returning to the case in question, things had not gone so well for our local builder attempting to produce the basketball court, destined to be the Lluidas Vale Sports Complex.

In the company of the builder and with representatives of the agency present, I conducted my field inspection. The basis of the dispute was that his work was found to be less than satisfactory, and payment had been withheld.

After hearing all the evidence presented at the site visit and returning to Kingston, I handed down my award within the promised fourteen days. Neither side got entirely what they wanted, but that is the nature of the process, isn't it?

11.

Bermuda

No respectable arbitrator should be allowed to confess that the job can be boring. But to be absolutely truthful, after sitting and hearing minor commercial cases involving matters unlikely to produce startling results or earth-shaking legal precedents, one falls into the inevitable trap of feeling a little jaded. This feeling may well be exacerbated, for example, by being geographically limited to practising in a relatively small island environment such as Jamaica's. The boredom increases exponentially when various attorneys quote the same authoritative cases or lines of quasi-technical arguments. One longs for something juicy and perhaps controversial to crop up.

While ruminating on the above, early in 2000 I received an enquiry from an old quantity surveying colleague of mine on another island. His associate, a US attorney, had been appointed to an arbitration tribunal charged with settling a dispute in Bermuda and was inviting me to participate as a member of the tribunal in a matter concerning a construction dispute in that country. When I heard "Bermuda", and knowing absolutely nothing about the place apart from what I had seen in tourist advertisements, my first thought was that it sounded a great deal more interesting than a dreary case in rural Jamaica.

Correspondence soon established that one member of the tribunal would be a gentleman named Harry Arkin. Neither of us had heard of him before, but we soon learned that he, too, was an American lawyer, nominated by one of the parties to the dispute. In due course we discovered that Mr Arkin was in fact a noted arbitrator in his own right, the principal of his legal firm in Colorado, and a prominent member of the US branch of the Chartered Institute of Arbitrators.

In subsequent trilateral discussions, I was chosen by the other members to be the tribunal chairman. At first, my natural sense of professional modesty inclined me to turn down this prestigious offer, but (as I preferred to think at the time), like Caesar, I decided to accept it before the others had a chance to change their minds.

In accordance with my custom in these situations, I began by establishing the jurisdiction of our tribunal. I suggested that this was a routine matter, to which my companions agreed – but for different reasons than I had meant. They took for granted that the jurisdiction was evident from the contract between the parties, whereas I believe that in an arbitration, no matter how simple or straightforward things may appear to be, nothing must be taken for granted without proof or confirmation. When this simple but fundamental difference of view between us became apparent, they asked me: "Well, what do we do now?"

Since we were unable to settle the terms of jurisdiction by informal discussion, I was requested, as chair, to mediate the issue on behalf of the tribunal. This proved to take rather longer than anticipated but, eventually, was settled to the satisfaction of all concerned. The jurisdiction of the tribunal was established after coming to agreement on most issues and finding a common ground for going forward. Not a smooth and easy task but one in which tact, patience and a smidgen of persuasion produced the desired result.

Having overcome this initial hurdle and committing the jurisdiction agreement to writing, my next task was to arrange a preliminary meeting in Bermuda. As always, the main purpose of this was to determine the parameters – procedures, rules, location, timelines of predetermined actions by the parties and the tribunal – of the conduct of the arbitration and its participants.

The meeting was to be held in the salubrious surroundings of the Hamilton Princess Hotel in the island's capital, with all parties in the dispute and others with an interest in the outcome present, accompanied by their respective legal representatives. The claimant, we were told, was a construction company that had been contacted by the respondent company, The Bermuda Underwater Exploration Institute, to build a museum that was, at the time of the hearings, in the final stages of completion. The legal team representing the claimant was headed by Mr Gerald Katz, a prominent US construction lawyer; the respondent's legal team was led by Mr Saul M. Fromkin, of whom we shall hear more later.

Contrary to general opinion, the Bermuda group of islands is not part of the Caribbean, nor is it similar in culture or economics. Instead, Bermuda is a group of subtropical islands situated in the Atlantic Ocean about 600 miles east of the coast of North Carolina, and about 950 miles north of Nassau. The country consists of the main island measuring twenty-two square miles, surrounded by numerous small islands, islets or atolls. The capital, Hamilton, is the home of a fully independent British-style parliament (the oldest, islanders are proud to point out, in the British Commonwealth outside the United Kingdom) and is strictly categorized as a British Overseas Territory, with a population (then) of about sixty-five thousand. Discovered in 1515 by a Spaniard, Juan de Bermudez, Bermuda witnessed no development until about a century later, when the British navy decided that it was an ideal strategic waypoint en route to the newly established American colonies – until, of course, certain events there in 1776 changed things. These days, the island's economy is driven mainly by commerce and tourism. Visually, it is a relatively unspoiled ecological region distinguished by "Bermuda pink architecture" and a particular item of male attire known as Bermuda shorts.

My main recollection of the preliminary meeting was being introduced to the respondents' attorney, the erudite Saul M. Fromkin, Esq., OBE, QC, FCIArb, FSALS, senior partner of the Bermudian firm of Mello, Jones and Martin. Mr Fromkin was not particularly tall, probably late middle-age, impressive with greying hair and a short well-trimmed beard. He was a former solicitor general and attorney general of Bermuda – and prior to that, holder of several judicial posts in the Canadian government. I believe he sensed that I was somewhat in awe, notwithstanding that I was chairing the proceedings, but in keeping with his generosity of spirit, he soon allayed this with his kindness and gentle humour. Indeed, as the most senior jurist present, he assisted and kept us on the right track.

At my instigation, and as agreed at the preliminary meeting, our next step was to jointly visit the site of the dispute. Clearly the construction of such a complex project (which included a working aquarium) was neither easy nor simple for the average contractor to construct. It was our job to assess this complexity in relation to the terms of the contract and within the scope of what was called for in the legal requirements of the agreement and the entitlements of both parties, and adjudicate on the additional values, if any, of changes to that agreement.

A trustee of the institute guided us through the incomplete project, which, although still lacking some essential non-construction components, such as water, fish and the like – was enough to give us a feel of what the Exploration Institute was trying to achieve. As representatives of both parties sought to call our attention to various items pertaining to their claims or counterclaims – at times emotionally – I felt the need to restrain them, reassuring them that the time for producing evidence would be at the hearing, not now.

"We are here to observe, learn and get as much of a 'feel' as possible for the project and for the case, so that we may understand the evidence presented to us in its proper context," I informed them.

The preliminary meeting continued the next day, with discussions and agreement about the procedures to be adopted in the conduct of the arbitration – timetables, presentation of evidence and so on, all as I have previously described and as prescribed by law (which in this case was the Bermuda Arbitration Act and the Bermudian Supreme Court rules accompanying it). Other matters covered were how communication between the parties and the chairman of the tribunal was to be handled; how witnesses were to be called and evidence presented; how the process of discovery and inspection was to be dealt with; and matters pertaining to the award itself, the tribunal's right to award costs and interest if so claimed, and the like.

When it was agreed that there were no more agenda issues remaining, I declared the meeting adjourned until commencement of the hearings at a later date, to be agreed between the parties.

Back at the hotel, the participants – now more relaxed than in the formal environment of the preliminary meeting – felt at ease to discuss a wider range of subjects: to exchange opinions on the current state of affairs in arbitration in our respective countries, the shortcomings of our different offices and the general and encouraging progress of alternative dispute resolution in the region. In this congenial atmosphere, and with consensus on the orderliness, beauty and peacefulness of Bermuda, we took our leave of each other and expressed our interest in meeting again in connection with this interesting case.

What happened next was unexpected but by no means unusual. In large and important arbitrations such as these, there is a tendency to believe that with "technical" judges, the length (and cost) of the hearings will proportionately diminish. In most cases this perception is true for the claimant and even more so for the respondent. It is only after the tribunal has heard all the evidence that the claimant intends to produce to support their claims (and by extension, the level of compensation or damages) that the two sides can reasonably assess the estimated cost of pursuing their claim.

In this case, the parties left my preliminary meeting with a much better idea of the anticipated cost of the tribunal itself – including the cost of transportation and accommodation for me and the other panel members in Bermuda, the cost of their legal representation and all other attendant expenses and costs – and after due consideration, they decided not to proceed with the arbitration after all, but to settle out of court.

Beyond the purely selfish disappointment at not being able to complete my social and geographical research of that delightful island, I was sad that I had not brought the matter to an arbitral conclusion. That said, just by having the parties meet face to face, making them aware of the strengths and weaknesses of their respective cases and of the cost of pursuing the matter to the bitter end, we, as a tribunal, may have brought value after all, to the parties and to the issue. I was curious to know how the case was concluded, but regrettably, we were not informed, and my file remained closed.

I should point out that what happened here is by no means unusual – particularly in jurisdictions where arbitration is practised freely and with no interference – and with the encouragement of the court, the percentage of cases settled before the hearings begin is high. There is no doubt that a properly structured and conducted preliminary meeting concentrates the minds of the disputants as well as of their advisers, which in turn may lead to negotiated settlements – as in this case.

12.

Garbage

This is a tale featuring much rubbish, both literally and figuratively.

As I mentioned in a previous chapter, the Spanish conquistadores who occupied Jamaica from the time of its discovery by Columbus in 1493 established their capital, or principal base, initially in a place they called Nueva Sevilla (New Seville), near the present north-coast town of St Ann's Bay. Later, they transferred their administrative capital to Spanish Town, in part to escape the intense mosquito infestation at their original location and in part to gain access to the natural harbour, which they named Porto Dogua. (It was then called Old Harbour and today is known as Port Henderson.) Following the British capture of Jamaica in 1655, the nearby Port Royal was deemed to be of greater strategic importance and emerged as a naval base and, more infamously, as the home port of privateers and pirates. A catastrophic earthquake in 1692 devastated the commercial and residential sections of the town.

While the naval fortifications remained comparatively intact, in order to accommodate the rapidly expanding commercial and strategic importance of the island of Jamaica, the government established a new capital across the harbour in Kingston. The new city prospered and was well laid out on a grid pattern with public squares and parks, as befitting the prosperity of the island at the time and its growing population.

The growth immediately before and after independence in 1962 was also a reflection of the region's increasing population and economic prosperity. The area known as Upper St Andrew – previously a sparsely populated rural area – was incorporated into the larger municipal area of Kingston and St Andrew. The main engine of its expansion was the burgeoning commercial private sector, which responded to the demand for land to satisfy the community's social needs. Developers competed for every piece of land available and, inevitably, disputes arose.

Which, lest you begin to think that this has morphed into a history or geography book, leads neatly to our story in question. In 1991, a dispute arose over a commercial centre development in St Andrew. In their search for affordable land, the developer came across a vacant lot in the Constant Spring area that suited their objectives, in terms of location and size, for a plaza of department stores, a bank, shops and offices.

However, those familiar with the area, which had witnessed other commercial developments, were curious when hoardings suddenly appeared around its perimeter. Speculation abounded as to its intended future use: surely, they said to themselves, it could only be a park or club or some such public open space, since – for as long as most of us could remember – everyone knew that the site had served as the region's rubbish dump. Once construction got underway and the site hoardings were removed, however, it became apparent that their speculation was wrong: they were presented with a new multi-use three-storey commercial centre.

My involvement in this matter began in mid-1991, when I received a letter from the claimant's attorney, Messrs Clough, Long and Company, informing me that a dispute had emerged between the developer and the contractor over alleged deficiencies in the construction of this project, and a writ of summons had been filed in the Supreme Court by the claimant (the developer) claiming damages against the respondent for breach of contract. The court, in its wisdom, had stayed the proceedings pending a court-ordered referral to arbitration, and that the two parties had agreed to my appointment as arbitrator. I replied that I would accept their proposed appointment, subject to my usual conditions (see practice notes 3 and 5).

It should be noted that, in most construction disputes, the terms and conditions of settlement by arbitration are usually spelled out in advance in the contract between the parties. If not, they may be incorporated by reference to a standard set of arbitral rules of a recognized body (such as the International Chamber of Commerce, the American Arbitration Association, the Chartered Institute of Arbitrators and the like). In this particular case, no rules were set out, either explicitly or by reference, which meant that I, as arbitrator, had to establish the relevant procedural and conduct guidelines of the arbitration before accepting the position. I did so, and, as in most cases, the two parties agreed to the terms (including the minor issue of my retainer fee).

I was able to proceed to my next step, the preliminary meeting, duly held in August of that year at the conference room of my office, which was big enough for meetings of this sort and similar small arbitrations (if not for major hearings, which were usually held in rented premises elsewhere). The respondent was represented by the Kingston law firm of Levy, Hanna and Company. Shortly after, I sent each of the parties my record of the proceedings. Although it is usually accepted that the arbitrator's word is law, in the interest of visible impartiality and the principles of natural justice, a reasonable arbitrator will always seek the parties' approval to his actions, and give them prior notice of his proposed actions, even if most of them had already been spelled out at the preliminary meeting (see practice note 6).

Two months passed, and I had not heard from either party in response to my record of the preliminary meeting, nor had they confirmed the dates for further action. This annoyed me a little, but since experience had taught me to expect much greater tests of my patience, I merely notified the parties that I was providing a fourteen-day extension for submission of their respective points of claim, else it was my intention to proceed with this matter *ex parte* (which, as noted, means that I would proceed in the absence of one or both parties). This is typically used only in the direst circumstances and is subject to reasonable notice given to both parties, but I thought it would help in this case, as in others like it, to alert the parties to their commitments pursuant to the arbitration timetable.

I was wrong. The two weeks came and went with nary a peep from either side. Feeling generous, I decided to give them a little more leeway and, allowing for the upcoming festive season, extended the extension until the new year (1992), thinking that this would suffice.

I was wrong again. Rather than conduct the arbitration *ex parte*, I decided to put away my files, but with the thought that I would certainly take this behaviour into account when in due course assessing costs while drafting my award.

I then went about my other business until – if this can be believed – one day in May 1993, I received a letter informing me that both parties of the dispute agreed fully with all of my preliminary meeting proposals and wished to commence arbitral proceedings immediately! Rome was not built in a day, I remember thinking to myself on reading this, but somehow I don't think that it was for reasons like this (see practice note 7).

Shaking the dust off my files, I gave the parties notice that the first hearing would be held on 22 August 1993. Within days of that date, however, I was contacted by attorney Mr Enos Grant, acting on behalf of the claimant, who said he had only recently been briefed by his client and needed more preparation time! Controlling my frustration, I asked the respondent if they had any objections to a further adjournment, and they had none (presumably, I speculated, because they too needed the extra preparation time). This extension, which I granted reluctantly, naturally had a knock-on effect on all subsequent scheduled dates of the proceedings, such as receipt by the respondent of the points of claim, their response and defence, possible counterclaims and so on. As it happens, a counterclaim did in fact arrive, which meant that I had to allow time for the claimant time to prepare their defence to that, and then for the respondent to reply.

At that point I decided that the charade must end and, exercising my authority as arbitrator, I established a strict schedule of dates for actions thereafter, with no exceptions or further extensions granted, so that the actual hearing could begin in November of that year.

In accordance with the outcome of the preliminary meeting, I was keen to conduct a joint inspection of "the scene of the crime". The operative word here is *joint*. First, to prevent any charge of bias should I visit in the company of only one party, and in case I should require explanations of any technical or other matters arising from my review of the case so far, the answers would be given in the presence of the other party. This, in my experience, is always a delicate matter for the arbitrator. On the one hand, it helps to get immediate answers to questions *in situ* that might otherwise take much longer to clarify at the hearing; on the other hand, granting this kind of latitude to the parties on an inspection tour usually gives rise to emotional attempts to argue the case there and then. An arbitrator's firmness is essential in these situations.

The bulk of the claims and counterclaims in the dispute concerned the cost of rectification of allegedly defective work – mainly sinking columns, sloping floors and the like – and a refunding of management fees paid by the developer to the contract–project manager for alleged mismanagement of the project. Cross and counterclaims flew back and forth throughout the proceedings like demented birds.

The site inspection duly took place, accompanied by many technical and legal consultants, each anxious to draw my attention to the parts of the project important to their case in terms of their respective contributions. As we walked past the entrance of the complex, I began to see the root of many of the claims made in the pleadings: walls were not straight; in many areas, floors, especially at the upper levels, sloped every which way but horizontal; finishings were of lower quality than one would expect of such a development; and there was serious settlement of various parts of the main structure. If I worked in one of these top floor offices, I remember thinking, I would need to take seasickness pills.

Occasionally in the midst of an earnest presentation there is a temptation to state one's own views – to offer advice, or benevolent guidance, to the parties. In this instance, I was sorely tempted to ask the presenters some basic questions about construction technology that apparently had been overlooked by both parties and their "experts" – for example, had no one taken into account that the differential settlement of the structure was possibly due to the fact that it was built on top of an old rubbish dump?

I was tempted, but as I had learned from many years of practice, it is important in such instances to bite one's tongue. Arbitrators with technical or practical experience and qualifications in a particular industry or scientific field have a greater duty of responsibility than those without: we must remember that *we are not witnesses – we are judges.* We must not in any way allow our personal expertise or training to influence our judgement of the issues put before us. Our duty is to arrive at equitable judgements based exclusively on the evidence put before us.

At the hearing immediately after the site inspection, attorneys on both sides made general presentations, supported by notarized witness statements from the experts, which were duly circulated to all concerned prior to the hearings, and their authors were asked to be present for cross-examination by the opposing side.

After ensuring that both parties were satisfied with the content and conduct of the proceedings and the completeness of their arguments and presentations, I closed the hearings on 23 December, in time for me to study the evidence and closing addresses of the parties at my leisure over the holiday season.

Six weeks later, I published my award, which was in favour of the respondent, the contractor. The issues were complex and the award well reasoned, I thought. In any event, the award went unchallenged by the losing side.

Postscript: Some time later, at a social function in Kingston, I met the claimant again, and, contrary to my anticipation of hostility, which one would expect from a losing party, he approached me most affably, expressing the view that my conduct of the arbitration was exemplary and that, in his opinion, my award was very fair indeed.

13.

Cricket, Lovely Cricket

Readers familiar with the geography of Kingston, Jamaica, will know that the home of Jamaican Test cricket is Sabina Park, in what is now part of the downtown core.

When founded in the mid-nineteenth century, the Kingston Cricket Club, as it was then known, was a small piece of open land at the rural outskirts of the city – ideal premises for a social club for the colonial expatriates of the time. After the First World War, Sabina Park hosted cricket legends such as George Headley and R. Slade Lucas, thereby securing its position as the premier cricket ground of the country. It became a Test cricket ground in 1930, when it hosted the visiting Marylebone Cricket Club team for the second Test in the West Indies' first home series. Headley's further successes in the run-up to independence in 1962 consolidated that reputation, and, in response, in the 1970s the club named the new south stand after him. With a capacity of just over six thousand, the venue continued to host major events until the end of the century.

In 1975, the International Cricket Council launched the first of its one-day international tournaments – dubbed the "Prudential Cup" in honour of its first sponsors, the Prudential Assurance Company of the United Kingdom – which were to be held every four years on a rotating venue basis. The 2007 tournament, the council decided, would be held at various venues throughout the West Indies, Sabina Park being one of them. To this end, the International Cricket Council would provide financial support to upgrade the cricket grounds at all the appointed venues.

The chosen West Indian countries all eagerly awaited the cricket event, agreeing on schedules for opening ceremonies, warm-up matches, competition matches and, finally, closing ceremonies, each country responsible for providing its own facilities to conform to International Cricket Council standards. In the case of Sabina Park, the grounds were to be upgraded to a capacity of twenty thousand spectators, with a second North Coast venue of twenty-five thousand (immediately dubbed the Greenfield Site) – for the opening ceremony and warm-up matches – to be constructed from scratch. In 2003, the budget allocated for Sabina Park, including cost of construction, was set at US$46 million.

And so it came to pass that the then prime minister, the Right Honourable Percival James Patterson, decreed that planning of the two stadiums was to begin immediately. For the Greenfield stadium, an undeveloped site was chosen in the parish of Trelawney, with financing and construction the responsibility of a construction company of the People's Republic of China. Planning and construction of the upgrades and expansion of the existing facilities at Sabina Park also got underway, though precisely how, or by what process, the architects and engineers for the project were chosen, I never was able to establish with any certainty during subsequent hearings. Suffice it to say, an overseas firm of consultants was engaged.

The renovations contemplated by this ambitious scheme called for demolition of the present eastern stand; erection of a new two-storey (later enlarged to three-storey) structure housing "sky boxes"; extension of the existing George Headley Stand and the administration block of offices and facilities; and replacement of the old Kingston Cricket Club with a modern players' pavilion, food outlets, indoor nets on the ground floor, and a modern press box at the north end of the grounds to house some five hundred journalists. The popular open-air mound was to remain but be improved for the benefit of younger spectators.

Whether by competitive tender or negotiation (here too, the process of selection was never made clear, but it did not, in my opinion, affect the issue at hand), a general contractor, Ashtrom Building Systems Limited, was selected by the employer, Jamaica Cricket 2007 Limited, and on 21 January 2005, a contract agreed on to the value of US$18,603,068.00 "or such other sum as shall become payable". Work began soon after that, and, from the evidence subsequently received, in November 2006, the original design team was replaced by a team of Jamaican construction professionals. The

certificate of practical completion was issued by the local architect member
of that team on 11 December 2006.

Early in 2006, during the India tour of the West Indies at Sabina Park, it was
reported (http://kwese.espn.com/cricket/story/_/id/23008751/work-progress
-sabina-park):

> Only 9500 spectators will be accommodated into the ground as welders and
> masons continue their operations, with the only exception being the stoppage
> of cranes. . . . . Jackie Hendricks, the former West Indies wicketkeeper and
> current president of the Jamaica Cricket Association, never tires of sending
> out pleas to the locals, players, media, asking everyone to "bear with us". It's
> all just a necessary evil as one prepares for the World Cup next year; all just a
> bad dream before the birth of a "magnificent stadium". . . . "We are a month or
> two behind schedule," said Wayne Reid, the chairman of the Jamaica Cricket
> 2007 World Cup Ltd.

Prior to that release, fans were told that it seemed probable that the Fourth
Test June and July would have to be relocated. A press release from Jamaica
Cricket confirmed the dire situation – based on their current level of
mobilization, staffing, and so on, read the statement, "The schedule is showing a completion date of February 2007."

Sure enough, as this report predicted, construction of the project did
not quite proceed as planned, nor at the pace required for a complex and
time-constrained project of this sort. Multiple variations and substitutions
became major issues, and complaints were made about lack of progress, lack
of information, subcontract delays and holdups in materials delivery. As
the evidence subsequently revealed, there was nothing particularly unique
about this contract, but as the list of unresolved claims and counterclaims
grew, it inevitably went to arbitration. Although they agreed that a sole
arbitrator would be preferable to a tribunal, the parties to the contract
were unable to agree on who it should be, and so, as stipulated by law, an
application was made to the Supreme Court of Judicature, which, by order
of the Honourable Justice Pusey and ratified by representatives of both
parties – Messrs Grant, Stewart, Phillips and Company, for the claimant,
and Messrs Vaccianna and Whittingham for the respondent – appointed
me sole arbitrator on 30 July 2008.

As an avowed cricket fan and taxpayer, I was well aware of the problems at Sabina Park from what I read in the press. Nevertheless, before accepting the appointment, I enquired as to the different points of claim and counterclaim, and the main issues at variance. I was informed by the claimant that these were all standard construction industry matters and – in response to one of my preliminary questions – that none of the arguments of either party turned on any points of law (which may have required me to seek external legal advice, and for which I would have had to receive prior approval from both parties). At that stage, I believed that the case would be easily resolved and not present any great technical or intellectual exertion on my part. Alas, neither my natural state of eternal optimism nor my crystal ball prepared me for what was in store.

In September 2008, I invited both parties to agree on a date for a preliminary meeting, which I suggested might take place in that month of September or October. September and October went by, however, and I received no response. Finally, in November, I was advised by the claimant that they had been unable to obtain any response from the attorneys for the respondent. Considering this nothing more than a minor inconvenience, I wrote once again to both parties, suggesting a series of possible dates for the preliminary meeting. This time, sensing that an additional incentive might be needed, I added that in the absence of response I would proceed *ex parte*.

After the deadline passed and I had once again not heard from either party, I issued an order for directions (another item in the arbitrator's toolbox that effectively means "Ignore this at your peril"), instructing both sides to appear at a preliminary meeting on a given day in December 2008. At the appointed date, the meeting was duly held, with the claimant's team, led by Ms Hilary Phillips, QC, present – but, bizarrely, no sign of the respondents, nor any reason communicated to me for their non-attendance. Containing my annoyance at this apparent snub, I asked whether there was, or had been, any problem with my jurisdiction in this matter. I was told there was none, that the claimant had no idea why the respondent was absent, but that I should begin proceedings "post-haste" nonetheless. I then made the following statement for the record, and to underline my impartiality as the appointed neutral party: "In the interest of natural justice, I will proceed with this matter and inform the meeting that no advantage must be taken by the claimant by virtue of this situation and additionally, a greater degree of responsibility is accepted by me in maintaining the balance of natural justice during the progress of these proceedings." The meeting then proceeded as planned, and dates were set for the various actions. In late January 2009, I received the points of claim, representing, as it were, the opening bat of the claimant's innings.

The following month, I received a rather mysterious letter from the respondent's attorneys, informing me that they had not responded to any of my correspondences "because we are not satisfied with the manner in which the claimant's attorneys-at-law secured your appointment".

As a further bombshell, the letter went on to say that the defendant, as a government company, was no longer carrying on business and had no funds other than those owed to the respondent, and that the company's chairman had had to seek guidance from the Office of the Prime Minister on how to proceed.

I sat back in my chair, shook my head in disbelief and pondered my next move.

One of the things an arbitrator must not do, under any circumstances, is to take personally anything adverse written or said to or about him. Some members of the legal fraternity seem to think that relative to judges, arbitrators are somehow lesser mortals, and while they would never dream of demeaning or insulting a judge, particularly in such a casual manner and with no evidence whatsoever, or refuse to recognize his authority, arbitrators are fair game.

I had already received a copy of the contract in this dispute, and reasoned that since it represented the complete agreement between the two parties, even if the period of the contract had expired or had come to a conclusion, the arbitration clause still was extant, and the contract therefore provided the necessary authority. Furthermore, it did not state that the respondent was a government company, and the only reference to the prime minister was to his being a witness to the parties signing the agreement.

After further study of the various aspects and possible scenarios arising from the respondent attorney's letter, I concluded that it was nothing more than a "smokescreen", and that I should soldier on. In my reply to the respondent's attorney, I remarked that "the court order containing my appointment does not refer to any constraints on the arbitral process by the present or future state of the respondent's company status".

Finally (or so I thought) a meeting was arranged and held at the end of April. Mr Vaccianna, the respondent's attorney, was present, as were those who had attended the meeting in December. In keeping with the surprising letter two months earlier, the respondent's attorney opened the innings by "bowling a googly": to wit, that he had been advised by the Office of the Prime Minister that representation in this matter would henceforth be undertaken by the attorney general, and that, in the interim, the chairman of Jamaica Cricket (2007) Limited would maintain a holding brief on behalf of the respondent.

During the stunned silence that followed, I collected my thoughts and composure, drew a deep breath and invited comments from the claimants. These were predictable, and were coupled with a request for me to proceed with the hearing and issue an interim award. I supported this request and ordered that the presentation be made at the second interim award hearing on 5 May.

In concluding this meeting I dealt with an earlier application by Mr Vaccianna to be allowed to withdraw from the case. I granted his request.

The second hearing was indeed held at the appointed date and time, with the respondent represented on this occasion by the deputy solicitor general and Dr Wayne Reid, a prominent civil engineer and chairman of the respondent company. This time, Ms Phillips, acting on the latter's behalf, opened the batting by declaring that no defence had been filed by the respondent – which, of course, I knew – and that in its place, the hearing would hear a representation from the Office of the Attorney General.

The deputy solicitor general began by arguing that the government was not a party to this agreement; that the solicitor general had discussed the matter with the attorney general, who then spoke with the Ministry of Finance; and furthermore, that the issue also needed to be discussed in cabinet. The Ministry of Finance, he went on, was therefore asking for an adjournment of the morning's proceedings for the government to look into this matter.

On hearing this, I remember thinking at the time that were this truly a cricket match and I the umpire, I would rule these balls played at the claimant's wicket as preposterously wide.

The deputy solicitor general concluded by stating the following: "It is unfortunate that these gentlemen [Ashtrom's executive officers] have come all the way from Israel and have been caused inconvenience for which we are indeed sorry, but as government functions, it must be discussed by Cabinet. We therefore request an adjournment of one month."

I will refrain from recording the response of the claimant. Whatever terms of speech you might imagine they uttered under the circumstances were close to reality. As there was little choice in the matter, however, it was agreed that the next meeting would be held at the end of May.

The appointed day duly arrived, and, with teeth clenched and fingers crossed, I opened the hearing by enquiring if the parties were finally ready to proceed. Alas, the deputy attorney general rose to announce that they were not. He then went on to explain to his incredulous audience that while the matter had been sent to cabinet, the finance minister, who was responsible for the presentation, was presently off the island. Accordingly, he asked for a further adjournment of approximately three weeks. Amid deathly silence, he slowly resumed his seat.

Frankly, I had not expected the respondent to stall yet again, and so I found myself inwardly assessing my role in the case, which, despite being conducted according to the standard rules of normal arbitral procedure, had now descended into a farce. I also realized that some quick thinking was needed on my part to quell the minor rebellion that I sensed brewing on the claimant's side of the table. While the weak arbitrator's option of allowing proceedings to take on a life of their own would result in their dragging on interminably, the "strong arbitrator" option, of exercising one's statutory right to bring the proceedings to a head by issuing ultimatums concerning time and non-observance of arbitral orders, could not only curtail proceedings but be detrimental to the compliant party. After all – I continued in my silent debate – the claimants were here to obtain relief, not merely to obtain a pyrrhic victory. Although there was no question that I was in charge, how could I exercise that power to uphold the principles of natural justice and ensure that justice was indeed being done?

I decided therefore to grant the additional postponement, while expressing my great disappointment at the inordinate delays incurred to date (see practice note 41), and noting that it would not be in anyone's interest for me to act intemperately – particularly since the claimant had not pleaded any great resistance to the three-week delay. With hindsight, I believe that this was the right decision.

At the fourth session, which took place at the end of June, we received the welcome news from the solicitor general – amid audible sighs of relief from the claimant – that the cabinet had at last met to discuss the issue and granted approval for him to represent the Government of Jamaica, and proceed with the arbitration. Ms Phillips, for the claimant, noted that this was a relief for her clients, who on previous occasions had made the journey from Israel to Jamaica in vain. She further expressed concern over a published newspaper article to the effect that certain funds owed by the Jamaica Cricket Board could not be paid and should therefore be written off.

With this obstacle out of the way, I suggested that the remaining time of this session be usefully employed to agree on procedures for the way forward. This was adopted and, after much discussion, the main hearing was scheduled for the following month – and it took place as scheduled. This time the respondent was represented by the solicitor general, and far more progress was made compared to that in previous sessions. The respondents then asked for an interim award with respect to amounts not in dispute, which I duly handed down, with, I thought, the consent of both parties paving the way for a smooth transition to completion.

Prior to the adjournment of this session, we were pleasantly informed by a senior partner of the claimant's firm, Mrs Denise Kitson, that Ms Hilary Phillips, QC, had been elevated to the bench of the Court of Appeal, and that, as a result, counsel for the claimant would henceforth be led by Ms Kitson. On behalf of all present, I extended our hearty congratulations to Ms Phillips and wished her well in her new position.

Two further sessions were subsequently held in rapid succession, dealing first with the claimant's final submissions, including further objections to published press articles, which, they said, gave rise to grave concerns should the final award ultimately be in their favour. In response, and for the first time, the respondent submitted a written defence, comprising mainly counterclaims and the solicitor general's rebuttal of the outstanding claims. This defence concluded with the remarkable statement that "We cannot accede to an interim award – you do not have the confidence to make such an award"!

I chose not to respond to this half-hearted attempt at a challenge to my jurisdiction, given that it was entirely unsupported by any arguments, and the fact that most modern arbitration rules do not permit challenges to jurisdiction once hearings have begun (Jamaica Arbitration Act 2017 *Challenge Procedures* cap. 13). After discussion of certain other outstanding procedural matters – none of which I considered to materially affect the main issue of the arbitration – and after ascertaining that neither party had anything else to offer or raise, I closed the eighth and final interim award hearing.

After due consideration, at the end of November 2009, I handed down my interim award, which found in favour of the claimant. It was a reasoned award, comprising 120 pages: a summary of the pleadings made on both sides; a precis of all salient evidence received by me; the award proper; my detailed reasons for the various sections of the award in relation to all points of claim and counterclaim; and, finally, a comprehensive set of appendices in support of my conclusions.

Some arbitrations, like the proverbial month of March, come in like a lion and go out like a lamb. The Sabina Park arbitration was such a case. Not long after my interim award had been published, representatives of the respondent – in perhaps a tacit recognition of my reasons for granting interim relief to the claimants – met with counsel for the claimant and agreed on a mutually acceptable final figure. This was then communicated to me, with the request that I issue a consent award for said amount. I speedily acceded, and stumps, as it were, were drawn early in 2010.

Postscript

This case is the second in my arbitral journey that received – unwelcomed as far as I was concerned – public interest. Sabina Park and the game of cricket has, for decades, been treated with great reverence in Jamaica and the Caribbean; accordingly, the upcoming Cricket World Cup matches and the construction of new national facilities attracted more-than-usual attention. As early as 2009, apprehension was publicly expressed concerning the pace and increasing cost projections of the various projects.

The *Gleaner's* banner headline in their issue of 13 September 2009 proclaimed, "Government Might Have to Find $1.4 Bn More to Pay for Sabina Park Refurbishing":

> Minister of Finance, Audley Shaw, on Friday disclosed that the Israeli-owned construction firm Ashtrom Building Systems has claimed this additional money for work it did on the headquarters of cricket in Jamaica.
>
> According to Shaw, the matter is being arbitrated. "He said that the government had been told that the cost of refurbishing Sabina Park originally was US$17 million (J$1.5 BN). However, Shaw said Ashtrom had made additional claims almost doubling the original cost to US$32 million (J$2.9 BN).

And this headline appeared in the *Daily Observer* of 25 September 2009: "$231M in Estimates for 2007 Sabina Upgrade: An additional claim from Ashtrom Building Systems Limited for construction work on Sabina Park, Kingston, to co-host the 2007 Cricket World Cup has added $231 million to the 2009/10 Budget."

In the end, although Jamaica did not fare well in the competition, the improvements were made in time, both to Sabina Park and the new stadium in Trelawny. The media exposure of the huge cost overrun and the subsequent arbitration soon faded into oblivion following the success of the competition, and a good time, as usual, was had by all.

14.

A Matter of Interest

The extreme eastern end of the island of Jamaica is made up of two adjoining but very different parishes. To the north, the parish of Portland: mountainous, lush and fertile and long since the home of high-end tourism, catering historically to wealthy European winter residents. To the south, the parish of St Thomas: geographically dissimilar, reputed to be one of Jamaica's most mountainous parishes, with many large and fast-flowing rivers, the economy traditionally marginal, based on sugar cane, banana and coconut production.

Typically, and ironically, the two parishes owe their notoriety in part to two famous men. Portland, for its flamboyant patronage in the 1940s and 1950s of that swashbuckling Hollywood actor, Errol Flynn, who paved the way for others of his ilk to patronize the area of Port Antonio. St Thomas, a century earlier, for the great Jamaican freedom fighter and now national hero Paul Bogle, leader of the famous Morant Bay Rebellion who heroically faced his English executioners in 1865.

The above sets the scene for an arbitration, for which I was appointed sole arbitrator, to settle a dispute arising from a contract to construct a low-income housing project in the township of East Prospect in the parish of St Thomas. The parties to the agreement of August 1995 were the owners of the land and long-established Jamaican electrical engineers and contractors Y.P. Seaton and Associates Limited, and the government-owned National Housing Trust – the former to construct and the latter to finance the construction of 259 houses.

During the course of the contract, certain disputes arose – none of which need to be related, since they do not affect the essence of this tale – which were dealt with in keeping with my standard modus operandi. A preliminary meeting was held, and schedules for service were set by me, agreed to, and largely kept by the parties. Hearings began on 6 June 2005 and were concluded on 10 June.

My specific terms of reference were to adjudicate on two remaining outstanding issues of contention between the parties: to determine, first, the amount of interest due to the claimant (the National Housing Trust) arising from their agreement, and, second, the quantum of profit due (if any) from the Trust to the respondent arising from the same agreement.

My award, in favour of Y.P. Seaton and Associates Limited, was published on 12 July 2005. I determined that based on the contract between the parties and evidence and arguments presented, no payment was due to the claimant, since no interest was awarded or claimed. My award therefore contained a value due to the respondent in respect of profit arrived at by me in accordance with my terms of reference.

Now, here is the main issue that I had to face. Normally, in keeping with my experience, if a claim is made by one party against another, the successful party also claims interest payable from the date of the award until settlement. That presented me with a great dilemma. The respondent, presumably thinking that an award of interest would automatically flow from an amount awarded, did not in submission actually claim the addition of interest. My terms of reference of April 2004 were specific in relating to "the interest portion of this statement", which referred to the claim and not the counterclaim. My dilemma was this: Should I award interest to a successful party if doing so would be in keeping with commercial practice, but if not specifically claimed for by the party in question? As one could imagine, I struggled with the answer to the question. Can an arbitrator include in an award that which is both obvious and part of normal commercial practice, but not specifically claimed as such?

In my award, I included a lengthy section of reasons (see practice note 27). This was so that all who had access to the award would know how I arrived at my conclusions. In this case, and in keeping with the above logic, I explained the reasons and stated that no interest was due on the value awarded to the respondent.

Predictably, the respondent did not take kindly to my position. They promptly filed a claim in the Supreme Court seeking an order that the question of interest upon the sum awarded be remitted to me, in accordance with section 11(1) of the Arbitration Act, on the grounds that I "fell into error" when I determined that no interest was payable because "none was claimed/pleaded". Although not exactly thrilled by the accusation of "falling into error", I was glad my point of principle had been upheld and was not challenged. The court, under the hand of Judge Marva McIntosh, J, remitted the matter to me on 22 January 2007 "to consider and arbitrate on the issue of interest on the profit awarded".

Conforming to this request from the court, I set about to review the submissions of both parties as to the value and rate of interest for me to take into account in making my supplementary award. Here, gentle reader, at the risk of repetition, I was faced with yet another dilemma. (Nothing is ever as simple, or evolves as calmly and smoothly in arbitration, as one would like to imagine!) Having arrived at the rate and amount, would I apply simple or compound interest to that amount?

As instructed by the court, I published my supplementary award on 11 May 2007, compounding the interest due from 30 October 1997 to 18 January 2007 and stating the awarded amount in favour of Y.P. Seaton and Associates Limited. In my reasons, I stated that I was aware of the current stated laws on the subject of interest as well as the various case precedents presented by both parties to me. I took into account the argument that imposition of simple interest does not reflect current commercial reality and that – as I understood the law – any award of costs must place the claimant in the same position as enjoyed by him prior to the cause of action – and certainly not cause him to benefit or suffer. I further mentioned that I had arrived at this position after deep consideration of the rule of natural justice.

Well, guess what? Correct. Following my supplementary award, an appeal was immediately filed by the respondent (the Trust), requesting the court to set aside my award, and stating that it should be remitted to me "to reconsider and arbitrate on the issue of interest in accordance with the Laws of Jamaica" on the grounds that I had [once again!] misconducted myself in awarding compound interest to the appellant in my supplementary award for lack of jurisdiction and in using the rate that I had in my compilation of that interest.

The case came up for hearing in chambers on 10 and 11 April 2008, and in a judgement delivered on 11 September 2009, the learned judge set aside my award of compound interest and held that "the arbitrator acted in excess of his jurisdiction in awarding compound interest on contractor's profit and thereby misconducted himself". The matter was then remitted to me by the learned judge to "reconsider the rate of simple interest to be applied".

A word here on the subject of "misconduct", which, on application to the court, is one of the reasons that an award may be either "set aside", meaning negated completely, or "remitted", meaning sent back to the arbitrator for re-examination of part(s) of the award.

Misconduct, then, does not mean that the arbitrator has appeared at a hearing improperly dressed, has just run off with lead counsel's spouse, or has consistently used inappropriate language during a hearing. There are a number of reasons accepted by the court that justify as "misconduct". Among these are the discovery that an undisclosed relationship exists between the arbitrator and a principal player in an arbitration; that the arbitrator has not dealt adequately with all matters referred to them; that an arbitrator has exceeded their strict terms of reference or pleadings; that the award has been improperly procured; or that the arbitrator has made an error of law on the face of the award. The law also allows for genuine "slips" to be corrected by the arbitrator if discovered after publication of the award.

Returning to the case in hand, the tennis match continued. On 23 December 2009, the appellant (Seaton) served an amended notice of appeal challenging the learned judge's findings of fact and law, which was argued by the distinguished Jamaican jurist, the Honourable Lloyd Barnett, OJ.

He argued that this case did not strictly require the court to render a decision as to the scope and extent of the power of an arbitrator at common law or in equity, or under the statute to award compound interest, because "the arbitrator did not base his decisions on those jurisdictions but rather on the contract between the parties so that the award stands or fails upon the question of whether the terms of contract justified an award of compound interest".

The learned judges in their hearing of this matter by the Supreme Court Civil Appeal (No. 133/2009) decided that the decision of the lower court was to be set aside and that my award of 11 May 2007 was to be restored.

I apologize for relating at length this, my last example of how the arbitrator – after pondering and cogitating long and hard – believes that the handing down of the award is the end of the matter. Usually it is, but not always. What one learns from this case study is that an arbitrator must first know the case thoroughly. The arbitrator must also know the strict requirements of the parties concerned and their rights and obligations under the law and in conformity with the principles of natural justice. Readers would have noticed that after publication of the award, the role of the arbitrator is complete – that is, *functus officio*. He may be called back only to correct minor errors or slips on the face of the award. An important lesson to be learned from this is to make absolutely certain that both the award and the reasons supporting the award "stand on their own feet". In the above example, I played no part in the "tennis match" that followed the handing down of my document. The appeal, counter-appeal and final appeal all took place without the involvement of the arbitrator. That is not to say that I lacked interest in the proceedings – far from it – but analyses of the contents of my award, subsequent arguments and counter-arguments by learned counsels, and, finally, their Lordships of the Appeal Court, all took place without my involvement. Naturally, I was both relieved and pleased to finally learn that the appellate court had agreed, and that, ultimately, my interpretation of natural justice was confirmed.

My happiness was sadly and abruptly terminated by the receipt of a request from the appellant for leave to appeal the local appeal court decision to the judicial committee of the Privy Council of the House of Lords. Gritting my teeth and taking a deep breath, I decided that I had no choice but to accede to their request. Accordingly, I communicated this to both parties and contemplated my next move. Without too much debate with myself, I decided that since this matter had been launched into the deep waters of the Privy Council, I could not defend my wicket without guidance. I asked each party if they would have any objection to my seeking the advice of senior counsel and asked that they suggest names of mutually acceptable people for me to retain (see practice note 30). They locked heads and agreed on Mr Garth McBean, QC, an eminent lawyer with whom I had had past dealings.

Many months later, I received a copy of the judgement of the Venerable Law Lords, addressed to *The Queen's Most Excellent Majesty*, In Council, by the clerk of the Privy Council, dated 11 November 2015:

> Having heard submissions from the Appellant and the Respondents we have agreed to report to Your Majesty as our opinion that
>
> 1. The appeal should be allowed.
>
> 2. Mr Stoppi's supplementary award under section 12 (2) of the Arbitration Act should be set aside and the matter remitted to Mr Stoppi under section 11 (2) in the light of the Board's judgment with a direction that his jurisdiction is limited to an award of interest on a simple interest basis and that he should reconsider its exercise, including the rates adopted, and
>
> 3. the parties should have 21 days in which to make submissions in writing on costs before the Board and below and on other consequential matters with a further 7 days thereafter in which to reply in writing to each other's submissions.

Her Majesty was pleased by and with the advice of her Privy Council to approve the report and to order that those charged with administering the Government of Jamaica and all others whom it may concern were to ensure that it was punctually observed and obeyed.

On receipt of the above, I resisted the temptation to send a thank-you note to Her Majesty; instead, based on advice, I convened a meeting with the parties to agree on the protocol to be followed, the first stage of which was for the parties to send me their submission of their respective cases. This was received by me some time later and was immediately followed by a shot across my bow of a missive vigorously claiming that one of the parties had included evidence not in the originating arbitration, and therefore inadmissible.

This was challenged, of course, with the demand for a hearing and consideration of whether this was legally so. My thoughts on this matter were *of course not*! If allowed, any new evidence would open up the narrow issue under my jurisdiction to a new arbitral process, with all its horrendous implications.

Before I had a chance to ponder too deeply on this new turn of events, another shot. This, the aggrieved party exclaimed, was a breach of justice and not a matter for the arbitrator to settle, but rather a matter of law!

This statement was followed by a demand for me to "State a Special Case to the Court" on the interpretation of the law regarding new evidence. The demand, strange as it seemed to me at the time, caused me, in the interest of utmost caution, to hotfoot it to Mr McBean yet again. He too shared my incredulity but, after consideration, advised me that I had no choice other than to accede.

The governing statute law in Jamaica then was extant for all the cases quoted in this book and, almost unbelievably, was not replaced until the passage of the current Arbitration Act of 2017. The arbitral community in Jamaica laboured Herculean-like with an archaic colonial law promulgated in England at the closing of the nineteenth century, with only minor periodic cosmetic amendments made from time to time – contrasting with, and blithely unaware of changes made to, arbitral legislation in all other progressive jurisdictions.

One such change, applicable to the legal culture of the nineteenth century but no longer in the twentieth, which mainly prompted England to completely revise its law as long ago as 1968, was the infamous section 20 – Stating Case for Opinion of the Court – which for historic interest is quoted in full: "The Registrar or any Special Referee, arbitrator or umpire may at any stage of the proceedings under a reference, and shall, if so directed by the Court or Judge, state in the form of a special case for the opinion of the Court any question of law arising in the course of the reference."

Apart from its total irrelevance to modern practice, historically it became a tool for parties in some cases to unreasonably delay the arbitral process. So it was, as I viewed it, in the case under review here. What followed was an appearance in chambers before Mr Justice Batts, who set a future date for a full hearing of the court. Both Mr McBean and I left shaking our heads in disbelief but very much aware that we would play no part in this until a judgement, which would be given to me in order to resume the referred arbitration from the Law Lords in London.

Being inured to surprises in this long and tedious drama, neither Mr McBean nor I reacted when we were informed by a joint letter from the parties that they had reached an out-of-court settlement – the details of which were not disclosed to us – and asking that I prepare a consent award using the wording of a prepared joint statement and send in our final fee invoices.

15.

Conclusion:
Arbitration à la Carte

Since this is a collection of personal reminiscences rather than a definitive history of the development of arbitration in this region, I would make one final comment by way of looking back. In the past, and long before the era of computerization, the duties of an itinerant arbitrator in the developing world may have been regarded as similar to those of a rural doctor – the doctor treating illnesses, the arbitrator dealing with disputes. Some arbitral responsibilities were commercial, some contractual, some simple enough to be decided at a construction site or an attorney's office – but all, be they large or small, hinging on the integrity and reputation of the arbitrator. In all these cases, the disputants expect, and usually receive, a binding decision made by a trusted local individual, not necessarily a lawyer or clergyman, saving them from going through the anguish, formality and cost of the traditional court system.

In this slim volume, I have selected only a sampling of the many cases in which I have been involved over the past forty-odd years. In these instances of dispute settlement – also known as "alternative dispute resolutions" – I have always preferred my role to be defined not as an alternative to any particular process, such as a traditional court of law, but as a distinct and civilized means of settling conflicts.

Requests for my services have come from various commercial, governmental or institutional sources, from lawyers representing clients in commercial disputes, directly from the court, or from organizations such as the aforementioned Jamaica Social Investment Fund, as a "final settler of disputes" arising from their contracts or commercial agreements.

Some critics might be concerned that being all things to all people in need of help in dispute settlement – particularly in small cases such as those described in the Hill People chapter – may recall the adage "haste makes waste", and cause natural justice to fall through the cracks. By and large, however, quick and straightforward dispute settlement is what both parties want, and, until now, in some cases decades later, no serious objections have ever been raised to any such awards of mine.

Many of us are aware of the intricacies of the practice of arbitration: we have studied the law, the practice of arbitration, the various forms of alternative dispute resolution and the myriad rules that go with them, and listened to wise old arbitrators relating their experiences. But just as not all medical doctors are destined to become famous surgeons, neither are all attorneys or arbitrators likely to be involved in multimillion-dollar or complex international arbitrations. Rather, parochial professional dispute settlers in the developing world must adapt to the needs of the community: while they must certainly be skilled enough and prepared for the heat of a courtroom battle at any level, they must also be aware of their obligation to the society in which they practise.

In Jamaica, as in many other former colonies in the Caribbean, arbitration has been used as the principal – and sometimes only – form of alternative dispute resolution for many years, practised in the main by attorneys as a reluctant adjunct to their traditional legal and court work. I recall discussing with legal colleagues some years ago the benefits of alternative dispute resolution as a means of arriving at quick and accurate awards in commercial disputes. The response to my descriptions and occasional words of defence of the process was usually a few mumblings of polite acknowledgement or bored acceptance. In addition, I often presented prepared papers on the subject at the invitation of various eminent private sector commercial organizations, such as the Chamber of Commerce, the Private Sector Organization of Jamaica and so on – always to be thanked profusely, metaphorically patted on the head, and told to be on my way.

It was the construction industry in Jamaica that spawned many of the contractual disputes in the 1980s onwards that began to change this perception. Many of these hinged upon complex technical issues, which organically led to long-serving industry construction practitioners such as the pioneering quantity surveyor Alex Twyman, engineer Dr Wayne Reid, and myself – plus one or two senior members of the legal fraternity who were familiar with Jamaican construction law – being called upon to arbitrate those cases. After observing several well-publicized disputes settled through alternative dispute resolution, the legal fraternity appeared gradually to come round to the idea that arbitrators were not merely ambitious amateurs seeking to infringe upon their territory, but rather were potentially valuable contributors to the judicial and traditional court system and would greatly assist to remedy the growing backlog of unheard court cases.

Finally, after much debate, it was decided that the time was right to formalize the alternative dispute resolution system. As a result, in 2007, in collaboration with the long-established Dispute Resolution Foundation of Jamaica (of which some of us arbitrators are longtime members), application was made to the Chartered Institute of Arbitrators in the United Kingdom for Jamaica to become an official branch. Under the guidance and tenacity of Dr Christopher Malcolm of the University of the West Indies, this was granted, and the Jamaican branch of the institute has since thrived and has spawned several chapters of its own throughout the English-speaking Caribbean.

Far from resting on our laurels, the new branch has since been busy, and was, in conjunction with the Ministry of Justice, engaged in reviewing the Arbitration Act, which dated back to 1900 and was in dire need of updating. This, happily, has been done and, based upon the UNCITRAL Model Law, came into operation in Jamaica on 7 July 2017.

Standard rules and procedures are also under review, also following the Model Law, as are standards of education and entry into the profession. Mention should be made of the successful and well-attended first International Arbitration Conference, held at the Faculty of Law, Mona, in Kingston during July 2015. Much work still needs to be done, but we are confident that, with the energy and goodwill of all concerned, the objective will be achieved.

My arbitral journey now is nearly complete. It has been long, sometimes arduous, but always rewarding in the retrospective sense of helping to introduce and develop awareness in this region of the benefits of peaceful dispute settlement as an alternative to traditional methods of adversity and conflict. My motivation, possibly stemming from a childhood in the environment of post–Second World War reconstruction, centres on the firm foundation of my Judeo-Christian belief. As it is written in Matthew 5:9, "Blessed are the peacemakers; for they shall be called the Children of God."

Part 2.

Practice Notes

Abbreviations to Notes

AAA	American Arbitration Association
CIArb	Chartered Institute of Arbitrators
ICC	International Court of Arbitration
UNCITRAL	United Nations Commission on International Trade Law

Practice Notes

Realizing that the insertion of a plethora of footnotes and endnotes into the text would be disturbing for the reader, I have assembled practice notes in this section. They represent explanations, definitions and reiterations of my personal arbitral experience. These notes are not intended to be encyclopedic but are included in the hope that readers may find them useful.

1. **Gibraltar Camp**: The origin of the name "Gibraltar Camp" came from an edict of His Majesty's government at the beginning of the Second World War to evacuate the British civilian population of its fortified entrance to the Mediterranean Sea to safety. It was originally planned to evacuate them to the French possession of Morocco, but following upon its capitulation of France to Nazi Germany, Gibraltans were denied that haven. Instead, His Majesty's government ordered the governor of Jamaica to hurriedly construct a camp for those shortly to arrive in Jamaica from Gibraltar. Although it was originally planned and constructed to house large numbers of people from there, in fact only a small number actually made it to Jamaica. Thus the "camp" provided ample room to later house enemy alien prisoners of war and other internees, later to be joined by Jewish refugees from Nazi Europe – all lumped together for the duration of the war.

2. **Arbitrator's behaviour**: On the matter of the arbitrator's behaviour in arbitration proceedings, the first and most important lesson I learned was that the overarching concept of impartiality – and conversely, freedom from bias or external influences – is paramount. This may sound trite, but it is surprising how often responsible arbitrators, no matter how experienced, will remind themselves of this basic tenant when occasion arises. I liken

the arbitrator to the conductor of an orchestra: a conductor ensures that the musicians each play their musical scores on their allotted instruments at the prescribed tempo and timing, and that each member expertly performs so as to produce a harmonious result.

On a more practical note, arbitrators – even if they know more or have had more experience than those pleading – must base their award exclusively on the evidence presented; they must receive the evidence of witnesses and the submissions of those pleading cases and form opinions only on them. If, as sometimes happens, the arbitrator, in an attempt to assist the process, offers advice or guidance on a particular technical or legal point, that must bring their calculations and reasoning to the attention of both parties equally.

3. **Jurisdiction**: There are cases of a disgruntled party attempting to challenge the jurisdiction of an arbitrator; it is important, therefore, to be aware that The Arbitration Act, Part 4 s.16, states that the arbitrator has the power to rule upon their own jurisdiction. Also, on a related point, it is well to appreciate that usually the arbitrator is held not liable for anything done or omitted from their function, unless that particular act or thing being complained of is done in bad faith. Finally, one of the difficult issues that can take place in a hearing is the natural tendency for the arbitrator to become emotionally involved in heated exchanges between participants; this temptation is to be avoided at all cost. Stay cool and, when all else fails, call for a short adjournment for the arbitrator, as well as the parties, perhaps, to cool down. An extension of the above advice is for arbitrators to be aware that, as judges, they are immune from being sued for negligence or other forms of action against them (typically by losing parties); however, they do owe a duty of care to the parties by whom they are appointed to act ethically and impartially, and consequently are liable to those parties in respect of any perceived or actual negligence. Another unwritten law related to those who judge others is that of natural justice, the two legs of which are as follows: a) no person can be a judge in his own case, meaning also that they should have no personal interest in the outcome of a case and should not be biased, and b) one must hear the other side, to the extent that all parties must be given the right to fully state their case. The concept of natural justice originates with the writings of the Roman Cicero in the

first century BC, in which it is recorded ". . . that there were certain legal principles that were 'natural' and 'high' not requiring any statutory basis" ("Notion of Natural Law" [1:20]).

4. *Custos rotolarium*: In colonial times in Jamaica, as in most other British colonies, the principal magistrate of a parish was appointed by the island's governor – as the monarch's representative – and deputized on all matters concerning the Crown. This office is still extant in Jamaica and is limited mainly to ceremonial duties delegated by the governor general, such as to make recommendations for the appointment and supervision of justices of the peace for the parish.

5. **Appointment of arbitrators**: Who may be an arbitrator, and how is one chosen? The short answer to the first question is anyone – normally a person of integrity and impartiality – who is mutually agreed on by the parties or pre-nominated in an agreement or contract, or selected by an appointing person named in a contract, such as the president at the time or the Institute of Engineers, et cetera. In absence of the above, they may be appointed by each side submitting to the other a short list of nominees; any name occurring on both lists is usually then appointed. If all else fails, an arbitrator may be nominated by an administering agency such as the American Arbitration Association (AAA), the International Court of Arbitration (ICC), the Chartered Institute of Arbitrators (CIArb), or by application to the court. In the case of a tribunal or dispute review board, each party appoints their own nominee, who together select a third person as their chair.

6. **Immunity**: To elaborate on a previous point, it is important to understand that arbitrators, as judges, enjoy the privilege of immunity from prosecution. The only remedy of a disgruntled party to an award, or the contents of an award, is to apply to the court to have it set aside or remitted to the arbitrator for specific amendment. This will be done by the court only in cases of egregious and obvious misconduct on the part of the arbitrator, or to reconsider specific parts of the award not considered by the court to affect the remainder of the award.

7. **First job**: Having been selected, and before accepting the appointment, the prudent arbitrator will find out something about the case. Who are the

main protagonists? What is the dispute about? The arbitrator would also ask: Do I have any present or past association or connection to either of the parties that might impede my impartiality or bias?

These questions give arbitrators elect a rough idea of what they are about to enter into, and ensure that they are not currently, nor in the past have they been, connected with any of the main participants. This avoids the embarrassment of having jurisdiction challenged or the award set aside or remitted for causes of possible bias. Another point here is that, according to most jurisdictions, once the arbitrator has been officially appointed (including acceptance of such appointment), this cannot be changed or the arbitrator removed without the consent or order of the court. Thus parties cannot frivolously, or otherwise, change arbitration midstream.

Alternatively, the following words, more applicable to international arbitration, may be used:

> I am impartial and independent of each of the parties and intend to remain so. Attached is a statement made pursuant to article 11 of the UNCITRAL Arbitration Rules of (a) my past and present professional business and other relationships with the parties and (b) any other relevant circumstances as the attached statement. I confirm that those circumstances do not affect my independence and impartiality. I shall promptly notify the parties and the other arbitrators (if any) of any such further relationships or circumstances that may subsequently come to my attention during this arbitration. I further confirm that I can devote the time necessary to conduct this arbitration diligently, efficiently and in accordance with the time limit in the Rules.

8. **Restraint**: I use the word restraint in terms of arbitrators avoiding the temptation, while listening to long, sometimes boring testimony, to make uninvited comments, contradicting or commenting on statements by counsel or witnesses. Where the arbitrator is as knowledgeable or experienced as the witness, or more so, there's the temptation to offer gratuitous comments, which may lead to accusations of misconduct and possibly to the court having to remit or set aside the award. Similarly, one is restrained from making statements that may be construed to be partial – for example, to suggest additions, omissions or corrections to pleadings or statements to be incorporated later in hearing notes. One should constantly remind

oneself that arbitration is not adjudication; the arbitrator bases decisions exclusively on that which the parties present to support their arguments, and does not assist the parties in arriving at a conclusion.

9. **UNCITRAL**: UNCITRAL Model Law, as defined by the Jamaican Arbitration Act, 2017, Part 1, s. 3(1) – applicable to both domestic and international arbitrations – is based on international commercial arbitration adopted by the United Nations Commission on International Trade Law, Vienna, Austria, on 21 June 1985, and the amendments adopted by the commission at New York, United States, on 7 July 2006, and adopted from time to time by the Government of Jamaica.

As arbitrator Dr Christopher Malcolm has observed, "The UNCITRAL Model has become the gold standard across the globe, and is the model that is most respected and accepted by end users at both local and international levels in progressive arbitration jurisdictions. In fact, implementation of the Model Law is now considered to be a minimum standard, together with the adoption of the New York Convention on the Recognition and Enforcement of Arbitral Awards, as a basis for good arbitral jurisdiction."

10. **Arbitration agreement**: The importance of creating this document before beginning any arbitral actions cannot be overstated. The agreement should be in writing and can be in the form of an agreement entered into by the parties prior to the arbitration, or contained in an order for direction issued by the arbitrator. Typical contents include the following: statement of relevant statutes and regulations affecting the arbitration; the contract or agreement from which the dispute arises, and, obvious though it may seem, the recognition of and a brief definition of the dispute; the powers of the arbitrator to proceed in the case of *ex parte* notices (see later note); rules dealing with communication between parties and arbitrator; arbitrator's preference in terms of type and submission of evidence; rules regarding site inspections; comments dealing with expert witnesses or testimony; consent by the parties to the arbitrator's right to obtain expert opinion (including legal, if necessary) as a cost to the arbitration; a statement that the parties have agreed to abide by the decision of the arbitrator or tribunal, and how and when the award will be handed down; and details of the arbitrator's fees and permissible charges and method of payment (for

example, by one party or shared). UNCITRAL Model Rules are comprehensive on the subject of arbitral agreements and have now been incorporated into Jamaica's Arbitration Act, 2017, part 2, s.7.

11. **Declaration**: In a more formal or international setting, a form may be used in the selection of a sole arbitrator or panel as a pre-appointment undertaking. The following is suggested as a typical format:

Name

Address for service

Qualification/experience

Have you previously acted for or represented any or either of the parties to this issue?

Are you currently connected with or engaged by any or either of the parties?

Have you been properly retained by the party who nominated you, and do you have their unqualified consent to act on their behalf in this action?

Are you aware of any matter, present or past, which could prevent you from acting in an unbiased and impartial manner if appointed arbitrator in this matter?

Are you completely aware of the responsibilities you will undertake as arbitrator?

Are you familiar with the relevant legislation of the location of the seat of this arbitration?

Are you prepared to travel from your home base to any location selected for the hearing in this matter?

Will you have the time to deal expeditiously and reasonably in this matter?

What is your hourly rate?

12. **Oaths**: Prior to any hearing dates, the arbitrator should be prepared – by judicious enquiry to the instructing attorneys of proposed witnesses – to ascertain, if their evidence is to be given under oath, which holy book is their preference. I usually keep two or three widely used such volumes in my office, just in case. The parties should also be aware that false evidence given under oath no longer is a civil matter but is viewed as criminal and may be treated by the arbitrator as such. The following wording is usual: "I swear by Almighty God that the evidence I shall give before this arbitration shall be the truth, the whole truth and nothing but the truth." Or if the witness wishes to attest instead of swear: "I solemnly, sincerely and truthfully affirm and declare that the evidence I shall now give before this arbitration shall be the truth, the whole truth and nothing but the truth." The law is silent on the matter of oaths, this being a matter for the individual arbitrator to implement should it be requested by one of the parties. In any event, as stated in Part 4, s. 16 of the act: "The tribunal may rule on its own jurisdiction."

13. **Preliminary meeting**: After settling the terms of reference and becoming familiar with the terms of appointment, arbitrators should ensure they have an accurate overview of the dispute and a working grasp of the issues involved, and that they are prepared to jump into the deep end of the arbitration. A preliminary meeting will then be convened.

The arbitrator should attend the preliminary meeting with a list of questions, pertaining to the details of the dispute, to be answered by the parties. (What follows is not a comprehensive list of questions and tasks, and arbitrators should add to this as necessary.)

From whence does the dispute arise? Contract clause or subsequent agreement? I obtain details and copies of the relevant documents from which these clauses came. This will be important later, should questions of the arbitrator's jurisdiction become an issue.

Who is the claimant and who the respondent? This becomes especially important when dealing with service of documents and so on.

Next, the arbitrator should identity and confirm addresses (both for communication and service) of person(s) representing the parties.

It is a good idea then to request a brief description of the dispute and its component parts (both for claim and defence) – not more than, say, two hundred words – and the approximate value of the issues in dispute. This information may help in estimating how long the reference will take and the amount of the arbitrator's retainer fee.

Will any of the pleadings reply on points of law? If so, I reserve the right to refer such matters to my own legal adviser (as a charge to the arbitration), the results of which, after receipt by me, will be available to both parties.

Do either of the parties want me to make a site visit? If at least one of the parties answers yes, I will establish the ground rules for such a visit.

Next, "housekeeping" matters are decided by consensus.

Do the parties wish any form of discovery? If so, and again after discussion and agreement, I confirm the procedure, for example, of effecting it electronically. Dropbox or other forms of transmission of bulky documents can be employed. If, as I have experienced in the past, communication from the seat of the arbitration to persons in overseas locations are required, Skype-type software may be allowed.

The arbitrator should also keep a register of attendees at both the preliminary meeting and hearings. A standard schedule handed out to all present before meetings commence will ensure that names and designations of participants are properly recorded; for those who are transient, dates and time of arrival and departure from the meeting should be noted. Such a schedule typically states the following: the title of the case, names of claimant and respondent and for whom they appear (which side), with space for their signature; and name of the organization they represent (in the case of witnesses). Although it is not, strictly speaking, necessary for the records, I usually append a copy of these attendance registers to my award.

At the preliminary meeting, arbitrators who are not attorneys or members of the local bar are advised to obtain consent from the parties to seek legal advice and opinion on matters of law that may arise during any of the proceedings. A typical wording in the first order for directions may include the following: "The parties agree to me obtaining legal advice which I may consider necessary either for my own edification or in connection with legal points or issues bought up in pleadings or evidence. Should any such points be brought to me by either party, they shall be submitted to me in writing; responses received by me will be communicated to the parties for their information. The parties should be further advised that the cost of legal advice will be a cost to the arbitration." At this stage, parties should be advised of the importance of strictly conforming to the established rules of the arbitral process and, when not observed, the penalties attached. (See the Arbitration Act 2017, s. 40.)

14. **Programme**: A vital component of this exercise will be the discussion – led by the arbitrator – on the matter of the parties' agreement to a timetable of arbitral events. Here, the guiding hand of the experienced arbitrator is usually appreciated by the parties, who naturally wish to gain as much time as possible to present their various pleadings.

Firm dates should be established for the service and response to pleadings and completion of all interlocutory proceedings.

Next comes scheduling of dates for the hearing itself. Again the arbitrator is advised to be "on the ball". Since attorneys prefer to juggle these dates to suit their court commitments, firmness is essential here, and the arbitrator should remind the parties of the high cost of prevarication. Other housekeeping matters will include, for example, deciding whether a court stenographer is required, and if so, who will bear the cost. I tell the parties that irrespective of their method of recording proceedings, I take my own notes, but these will not be available to the parties (unless, in the case of appeal, I am ordered by the court to make them so).

It is also important to establish how many expert witnesses will be called, and what the details are of their qualifications and subjects to be presented, as well as the location of premises for the hearing, details and scheduling thereof, and costs involved. I also ask for a properly indexed and paginated "bundle" to be agreed on by the parties and presented to me prior to the hearing.

Finally, and importantly, the arbitrator should prepare a statement of the fee, how it is to be calculated and how expenses will be dealt with.

The arbitrator should prepare the notes of this preliminary meeting and request confirmation of them from the parties.

15. **Pleadings**: Put simply (indeed, entire books have been published on this topic alone), pleadings are documents exchanged before the hearing and submitted to the arbitrator, setting out the basis of claims and rebuttals

and/or counterclaims and attempting to substantiate the parties' contentions and opinions that they hope will sway the decision in their favour. These may also contain any basic facts or points of law upon which arguments will be based, though no evidential material is included at this stage. This exercise ensures that the respondent knows what case they are expected to answer, and that the claimant is aware of the main points of defence. It also avoids surprises (or "ambush" techniques) during the hearing. Usually I allow reasonable amendments to pleadings to be made at any time up to, but not after, the hearing commences. Here, the arbitrator needs to be vigilant in not allowing substantial differences, disguised as evidence, to be introduced into pleadings after the hearing has begun.

16. **Reluctant parties**: In cases where an arbitration requires a sole arbitrator or a tribunal and the parties do not concur in such appointment; or if the appointed arbitrator declines to act or dies, and the parties do not appoint a substitute; or, where two arbitrators refuse to appoint an umpire, then according to the current Arbitration Act, s. 6, "Any party may serve the other party or arbitrator, as the case may be, with a written notice to appoint such an arbitrator, umpire or third arbitrator. If the appointment is not made within seven days after the service of the notice, the Court or a Judge may, on application of the party giving notice appoint an arbitrator who shall have the like powers to act in the reference, and make an award as if he had been appointed by consent of all parties."

17. **Expert witness statements**: The principle of witnesses providing testimony on technical or trade practice matters germane to the arbitration, is that they do so not as agents of those who employ them but as having an overriding duty to the arbitration (or court) by those presenting such reports. The following is a defining statement guiding potential experts providing such testimony: "It is the duty of the expert witness to assist the Court (arbitration) impartially on the matters relevant to his/her expertise." Hence, the evidence, always in writing, must be objective, free of bias or preference, concise, and, above all, able to be challenged and defended on content by opposing arguments. Such evidence does not have to be orally presented and may be subject to cross-examination. Most jurisdictions have civil procedure rules governing this subject (Jamaica Civil Procedure Rules,

part 32) and covering the behaviour of experts and assessors, and these rules are usually extremely comprehensive; to repeat their content here would be both tedious and repetitious.

Some cases contain much technical data or calculations, the argument of which before the arbitrator will be unnecessarily time-consuming and possibly repetitious. It has been found recently that the pre-agreement – between competing experts or assessors – of non-disputed results of calculations or other facts is beneficial to the arbitration. The end product of this will be a concurrent expert evidence submission, signed by both sides and signifying points upon which there is no longer a dispute. It is claimed that this process saves time and costs, improves the quality of expert evidence and assists the arbitrator in understanding complex issues. In the United Kingdom, this process, for some strange reason, is known as "hot tubbing". Another variation of hot tubbing allows the disputing experts to appear jointly and be sworn in together at the hearing, so that conflicting interpretations of fact can be debated by presenters of the expert evidence, cross-examined by the other side and even questioned by the arbitrator. Caution must be engaged by the arbitrator in controlling this exchange to avoid any abuse of this privilege.

18. **Scott Schedule**: Of interest to those involved in technical or complex cases is the requirement for parties to agree to a Scott Schedule, sometimes referred to as an official referees schedule. The accepted form of this schedule provides two sets of columns identifying separate points of claim or counterclaim, each set with columns headed *Details* and *Amount* with separate columns headed *Claimant's response* and *Arbitrator's notes*, each entry properly indexed and cross-referenced. I have saved much time and frustration using this method during and following a hearing and when tabulating reasons for the award. A typical form may be as follows:

In the Matter of an Arbitration

Between

Company X – the Claimant, and

Company Y – the Respondent

Scott Schedule made in accordance with Arbitrator's Order for Direction No. X Dated . . .

Item No.	CLAIMANT	RESPONDENT'S REPLY	CLAIMANT'S RESPONSE	ARB'S NOTES
X	Details	Amount	Details	

19. **Redfern Schedule**: In more complex cases, or in international arbitration containing a plethora of information or documents to be exchanged, accurate records of requests for information or documents and responses to those requests may be encapsulated into schedule form, so named after the author of such forms, Alan Redfern. Details of a typical form containing six columns, headed with the case identification followed by the name of the requesting party, are arranged as follows:

1. Reference number and date of request
2. Specific document or category of documents requested
3. Relevance and materiality according to requesting party:
   (a) Reference to Submissions, Exhibits, Witness Statements or Expert Reports
   (b) Comments
4. Response or Objection to request(s)
5. Reply to Objections to document requested
6. Decision of Tribunal or Arbitrator

20. **Confidentiality**: Mention was made earlier that there should be a degree of confidentiality in the conduct of arbitration. Easier said than defined. One of the principle features of arbitration, and certainly one that appeals to commercial litigants as compared to litigation in court, is not necessarily secrecy but a degree of privacy. This may particularly apply in cases involving propriety trade processes, or where, in the opinion of the arbitrator, disclosure of a particular item may cause embarrassment or disadvantage to one side without detriment to the other. Arbitrators, while respecting the need for confidentiality, should be aware of the power of the court to override the implied obligation of confidentiality. The term *implied* is used deliberately, since the question of confidentiality is mentioned neither in

any local legislation nor in the English act of 1996. As always, it is up to the arbitrator to ensure a judicial balance.

21. **Closing addresses**: Usually in cases involving detailed points of claim, responses and possibly counterclaims, parties or their representatives are permitted to summarize issues that arose during the hearing in order to sum up their positions in closing addresses to the arbitrator. The purpose is for the parties to persuade the arbitrator why the facts presented support their side. The general rule is that the respondent goes first, followed by the claimant, who will have the last word.

22. **Closing the hearing**: After receipt of closing addresses, the arbitrator will ask the parties or their representatives if they wish any other matters or points to be heard; this is to ensure that the parties are satisfied that all matters contained in the arbitration agreement or subsequently introduced have been adequately dealt with. It is equally important for the arbitrator at this stage to ensure that no matters included in the award are in excess of his jurisdiction. Arbitrators should be aware that either of those departures from the strict terms of reference to the issue, however innocent, may be cause for an aggrieved party to accuse the arbitrator of "misconduct". The arbitration agreement will usually state the time allowed for the arbitrator to hand down (or publish) his award. If not so stated, it will probably have been included in the notes of the preliminary meeting. The time for the production of an award is usually left to the arbitrator. I stipulate "within three months", but this period may be extended if required.

23. **The award**: An arbitrator's award should exhibit the following characteristics:

- be concise and to the point
- be relevant, covering all the points raised both as claims and counterclaims
- exclude references to all matters not raised as such
- be in writing, and signed and dated by the arbitrator in the presence of a witness
- be handed down by the arbitrator within the time specified by law or the arbitration agreement

- be certain, unequivocal, and neither capable of different interpretation nor ambiguous
- must deal with all items submitted and exclude any not so pleaded
- be final and binding on the parties named
- be clear on the remedies awarded and, where applicable, interest awarded
- contain just enough recitals to identify the genesis and nature of the dispute
- state reasons for the details of the award
- where required by the agreement or law, award costs arising from the award
- be enforceable in the same manner as a judgement of the court

There are two other sorts of awards: consent awards and interim awards.

Consent award: Where the parties to a dispute, at any time after signing an arbitration agreement and before the publishing of an award, agree on a settlement or simply to abandon the proceedings, the arbitrator, acting in accord with the written agreement of the parties, may issue a consent award reflecting the terms of the parties' agreement and bringing the process to an end.

Interim award: Where a specific matter or item contained in the body of a greater issue needs to be settled for reasons of great urgency, and by the agreement of the parties, an arbitrator may conduct a "mini-hearing", the award of which may then be incorporated into the main award as a settled item.

24. **Awards for specific performance**: These are rare and only applied where such a remedy is pleaded and also where an award for the payment of a sum is inappropriate for the restitution of natural justice. All awards must be worded and handed down by the arbitrator in a form that is capable of enforcement or judgement of the court. Unless otherwise stated in the award, interest will accrue from the date of the award at the same rate as a judgement debt.

25. **Sealed offers**: In the same way offers and counter-offers may be made by the parties – prior to the closing of the hearing – to effect an intermediate settlement rather than pursuing the arbitration to its bitter end, so may one party make, to the arbitrator, in a sealed envelope, a record of an offer

to settle which had been refused by the other party. The sealed envelope is opened by the arbitrator after reaching the award but before deciding on the award of costs. If the party's offer is found to be more than that of the arbitrator's award, then, most likely, costs will be awarded against the refusing party because if the offer had been accepted, the arbitration would have ended then, thus avoiding a substantial portion of costs. There are many variants to the above, a bit too complicated to discuss here. One variant worthy of mention is a Calderbank Offer. This is where a party makes a sealed offer *after* the arbitrator has considered the substance of the award; in this way parties are given an opportunity to address the arbitrator on the matter of costs before they are awarded. (*Calderbank v. Calderbank* [1975] 3 All ER 333 – later *Cutts v. Head* [1984] 1 AER 597.)

26. **Template of a typical award (suggested):**

Reference:	Relevant arbitration law; correct names and description of the parties, their representatives and others appearing at the hearing; type of contract or agreement and reference to the arbitration clause from which this action originates.
Dispute:	Type of dispute; details of arbitration rules used – standard, e.g., UNCITRAL, ICC, AAA, CIArb or ad hoc; arbitrator's appointment and jurisdiction; seat of the arbitration; which party is claimant and which respondent.
Proceedings:	List orders for directions and other instructions given; outline of pleadings served; date and brief outline of hearings held; site visit details, if applicable; schedule of witnesses and production of other key evidence.
Issues:	What is claimed and counterclaimed; law involved, if any; upon what has the arbitrator been asked to rule; has specific performance as well as other remedies been pleaded, if so – details.
Award:	Be the style and type required by the arbitrator agreement; give awarded amounts (if applicable) to each item as pleaded; give reasons for all parts of the award and clearly state who is to pay, how much and to whom; deal with interest and award of applicable and allowable costs; state arbitrator's fees and expenses

and – most important – attach arbitrator's invoice to the award; finally, state that all matters have been dealt with and that this award is in full and final settlement.

Upon publishing the award, the job of the arbitrator is usually over, characterized by that delightful legal term *functus officio*.

27. **Reasons**: According to the Arbitration Act, s. 31(3), arbitrators must state the reasons upon which the award is made – not, please note, the "reasoning" for arriving at their decisions. These become important mainly for the parties to understand why the award contains the decisions stated and for those pleading their cases to understand the logic of the decisions made, to help in enabling the parties to continue their commercial or other relationship. Finally, should the award be challenged, to help an appeal judge to understand the arbitrator's thinking.

Usually, at the end of the hearing, the arbitrator will conclude by saying nice things about those who participated in the arbitration and – hopefully – nice things will be said in return about the arbitrator!

28. *Ex parte*: Translated from the Latin, this term meaning "by or for one party" or "by one side" is usually interpreted as the proceeding of ordered events in the absence of one of the parties. Typically it is used by the arbitrator to prevent one side from unduly or unreasonably delaying or obstructing the arbitral proceedings, such as by refusing to attend a scheduled hearing or persistently refusing to conform with arbitral orders or production of documents required for discovery. In order to impose this rule, it is vital for the arbitrator to give reasonable notice to the offending party that it is the intention so to do. It is only necessary for this notice to be given once, hence advisable to issue a notice equally and simultaneously to both parties where repetition of the offence is likely to reoccur from either party. Since this strategy can be challenged, it is prudent to include in the order following the preliminary meeting such a general notice, hoping that it will prove unnecessary

29. **Qualities of an arbitrator**: Although not specifically dealt with in the text, it would be appropriate to further comment here on the required qualities of an arbitrator. Suffice it to say that they ought to be confident of their

ability in terms of the overriding law and applicable regulations as well as their knowledge of the issues in dispute to be able to equitably and fairly – but only on the basis of evidence adduced during the proceedings – arrive at an unchallengeable award. There will be moments, in the heat of a contentious hearing, perhaps, when the arbitrator may feel intimidated by legal counsel or an overbearing witness. Such intimidation is to be resisted at all costs. The arbitrator is in total charge of the proceedings and has the same power as an officer of the court; as such, the office of arbitrator is to be respected, not abused. Personally, I have not had occasion to use it, but a charge of "contempt of arbitration" bears the same weight as "contempt of court"!

30. **Legal advice**: Arbitrators, especially non-attorneys, are entitled to engage the services of a legal adviser or counsel, to provide advice and assistance on any legal issues that may arise. Such advice is limited to factual matters and opinions unclear to arbitrators and required by them to arrive at their decisions. In such cases, all such questions put to counsel should be in writing, and both questions and answers should be submitted to the parties. When an arbitrator receives a "no objection" letter from an attorney, it may be incorporated into the arbitrator's award. Alternatively, such advice may be incorporated in a reasons section as part of the award.

31. **Incorporation by reference**: A word of caution on referring to other documents in arbitral awards, either to prove a point or, by quoting a clause in a contract or agreement, to reinforce a decision of the arbitrator. It should be made clear that any reference to another document is to highlight a specific point or clause, and not, under any circumstances (unless so intended), to imply that the whole of the text of that document is being accepted.

32. **Appointment of arbitrators (2)**: A further word on the appointment of arbitrators and how they may obtain their authority: by pre-nomination in an agreement or contract; by nomination by an administering agency, such as AAA, ICC, CIArb or by the court. In such cases of administered arbitration, standard and published procedures will be followed. In the case of private or ad hoc arbitration, the usual custom is for both parties to produce a list of preferred arbitrators and, by comparison, appoint from

those that coincide – if not, they may continue the process until selection is achieved or by reference to a stated nomination agency (for example, the president for the time being of the Jamaica Institute of Engineers) or, again finally, by the court. If no such appointing agency is stated in the agreement, then by application to the court. In the case of a tribunal or dispute review board, each party appoints their own nominee, who then selects a third person as their chair, third arbitrator or umpire.

Next, having been selected and before accepting the appointment, the prudent arbitrator will find out something about the case. Who are the main protagonists? What is it roughly about? This is to get an approximate idea of what the arbitrator elect is about to enter; is he or she connected – either presently or in the past – with any of the main participants? This caution is advised to avoid the embarrassment of having jurisdiction challenged or the award set aside or remitted for causes of possible bias. Another point to note here is that, according to most jurisdictions, once the arbitrator has been officially appointed (including their acceptance of such appointment), they cannot be changed or removed without the consent or order of the court. This also means that parties cannot, frivolously or otherwise, change arbitrators midstream.

33. **Defaulting party**: The act deals with this matter at s. 40 and states that if without showing sufficient cause the claimant fails to communicate their statement of claim in accordance with s. 38(a), then the arbitrator shall terminate the proceedings. If a party fails to appear at a hearing (subject to proper notice having been served) or fails to produce documentary evidence, then the tribunal may continue the proceedings and make the award on the evidence before it.

34. **Arbitrator's fees**: For the inexperienced arbitrator, this may be a convenient point at which to pause and discuss the matter of arbitrator's fees. From experience, I have found that avoiding or deferring discussion of fees with the parties (or appointing authority), for the sake of diplomacy or any other reason, is ultimately detrimental to the process. Most significantly, it results in the arbitrator being unable to budget properly. Normally the arbitration agreement will contain details of the arbitrator's charges, based on an hourly or per diem basis. It should also be possible to roughly assess

the length of the process by projecting time to be spent on site visit, preliminary meeting, hearing(s) and study of documents and evidence. By calculating an approximate gross time value, plus anticipated and normal expenses, an arbitrator can estimate the total fee.

One reason for doing so is to request a retainer fee based on, say, 20 per cent of the estimated fee, one half to be paid by each party and deducted from any future billing. If the process is anticipated to be lengthy, for example, if it involves overseas travel, the arbitrator can request that interim invoices be submitted and paid. Should the matter be withdrawn or settled before the hearing stage, it is usual to state that 50 per cent of the retainer fee will be returned. The arbitrator will break down the final fee invoice to show the time spent on discrete activities and include a detailed statement (with receipts) of the claim for "normal and reasonable" reimbursable costs.

The value of this invoice will be stated in the body of the award as a cost in the arbitration with directions for payment – for example, by whom, if it is to be paid by one party only, or in what proportion, if it is to be shared. Having been "bitten" once by an unscrupulous party to an arbitration, I require that the invoice be settled before releasing the award. In cases where interim payments have been made equally by the parties, a typical clause following the statement in the award of fees due may be as follows: "I further award and direct that if the claimant/respondent shall have paid all or any of the costs of this my award he/she shall forthwith be reimbursed by the other party the full amount so paid."

35. **Third-party funding**: In certain large, complex, international or intra-government arbitrations, costs can escalate to a point of unbearability for one party or the other. Notwithstanding the justness of a litigant's case, the depth of his pockets may determine his staying the course of natural justice or not. In such cases there now is a growing tendency for a third party – not a party to the dispute – to offer a party litigation funding in return for a percentage of the award, and agree to receive nothing if the claim fails. The ancient word for this type of action is *champerty*. Much debate surrounds this system. Although not illegal in most jurisdictions, it raises issues of impartiality, confidentiality, undue influence of funders on procedures, problems of award of costs in connection and so on.

36. **Consent order**: A useful tool in the arbitrator's toolbox is the consent order. Once an arbitration process has properly begun, procedure must be in accordance with the law, the requirements of which will vary for each arbitration seat. Normally, the arbitration agreement will require the arbitrator to conclude the process by handing down an enforceable award. But what happens if the parties, after commencing the hearing and by mutual consent, wish to omit or change any of the pleadings? Providing this is not contradicted by the arbitration rules accepted by the parties, their wishes can be met, in the case of interim changes or omissions or additions, by the issuing of a consent order. This order has the same power as an order for directions, or, in the case of the parties wishing to agree, for any reason, the power to conclude the process. An application may be made to the arbitrator to issue a consent award. For a consent order, all that is needed is the signature of the arbitrator. For a consent award, the arbitrator is advised to state the logic and the reasons involved and, most important, have the order signed and witnessed by both parties prior to being handed down as a final award.

37. **Seat of the arbitration**: The term seat of the arbitration refers to the judicial place of the proceedings and therefore defines the applicable law. It need not necessarily be the location of the action, for example, in the case of shipping, or multinational or transnational commercial disputes. This issue should be brought up and incorporated into the arbitration agreement prior to commencement of the proceedings, to avoid uncertainty later regarding the applicable law. The seat can be established either by agreement of the parties, as stated in their contract from which the dispute originates, or by the regulations of an agreed institution such as the International Chamber of Commerce, or, as a last resort, by the court with jurisdiction over the dispute.

38. **Evidence**: Arbitrators should be wary, during the pleadings process, of haphazard presentations that do not deal directly with the matters supporting the arguments. Presenters who are not properly briefed, or who are unaware of the core issues, may, wittingly or otherwise, obfuscate the hearing to cover their deficiencies. In such cases, arbitrators must immediately correct the offender and bring the evidence back to relevance, while

being careful not to inhibit or intimidate. The matter of witnesses giving evidence under oath or not is usually up to the arbitrator.

Evidence of fact must be what a witness has seen or heard; presentations straying from this fundamental rule, for example, repeating what someone else has said or done, are considered hearsay and therefore non-admissible. The guiding principle of presentation of oral evidence is that the party who makes an assertion has the burden of proving it. The rules of evidence in arbitration tend to be more lax than in the court – and the degree of latitude, as always, is at the discretion of the arbitrator. The procedure of examination-in-chief followed by cross-examination is normal in arbitration. Arbitrators should ensure cross-examination questions are only in response to statements already made or presented.

Generally, only original documents are allowed as evidence, although in some cases arbitrators will allow copies if satisfied of their genuineness, or where such copies have been notarized. Most modern quasi-regulating agencies, such as the International Centre for Settlement of Investment Disputes, AAA, ICC and UNCITRAL, have published rules concerning the admission and use of electronic devices for presentation of evidence. If any such rules are contemplated in the agreement between the disputing parties, prudent arbitrators will satisfy themselves prior to allowing pleadings or presenting evidence. Evidence, particularly in international arbitrations, may be given by affidavit, written statements made by a competent witness to confirm facts or a particular document. The main difference between an affidavit and an expert report is that the affidavit is required to be notarized and may, subject to the discretion of the arbitrator, be cross-examined.

39. **Points of law**: All persons in charge of judicial proceedings, where their awards are expected to be accepted by both parties, are, as a matter of natural justice, expected to have at least a working knowledge of the statute and case law of the region in which the seat of the dispute has been established. The arbitrator is advised that, in the course of presentation of arguments, when points of law are introduced, the party presenting such points should be requested to submit them in writing to the tribunal. Clearly that presentation will include the logic of the application and case references, where applicable. The arbitrator then has the choice to rule on the application, or, in the case of technical arbitrators, to refer the legal point raised to an

attorney to whom neither party has any objection. The parties should, at that stage, be advised that the cost of such legal consultation will be dealt with as costs of the arbitration. Following the consultation, and the handing down of an unchallenged decision, it may become part of the submitting party's pleadings.

40. **Bundle**: A word of explanation regarding the "bundle". This is usually prepared following the process of discovery. The parties involved have a right to know in advance which documents will be presented at the hearing. In the process of discovery, then, before the hearing, each side simply provides the other with a list of documents, invoices, letters, variations instruction orders and so on. The process is usually initiated by one party requesting a list of relevant documents which are, or have been, in the possession of the other, followed by an exchange of such lists between the parties. All documents may be requested except those classified as "Privileged", such as those marked "Without Prejudice" or correspondence exchanged between a party and their attorney in anticipation of arbitral proceedings. After completing the exchange of lists, either party may request copies of any documents so discovered (subject to the reimbursement of the cost of reproduction). All are then bound in one book – one copy of which is provided for each party and one for the arbitrator. Arbitrators must be careful to supervise this operation to ensure that all documents are included, properly indexed, numbered and cross-referenced. Otherwise, confusion and lost time will reign during the hearing. One of the benefits of the bundle is that it introduces discipline into the process of production of evidence. Additionally, it prevents delay during the hearing if either party challenges the introduction of a piece of evidence. It limits the time taken for discovery and makes the production of evidence and the process of examination and cross-examination more efficient.

Tip: Request and keep a soft copy of the bundle (as well as the award, by the way) in a safe place, just in case the unthinkable happens and they are lost or destroyed.

41. **Delay**: Of further interest to practitioners is the arbitrator's right to deal with long drawn-out cases. Currently there is no specific provision in the law that allows the arbitrator to grant an injunction preventing claimants

proceeding in the reference, when they have been guilty of inordinate delay in pursuing the matter. Nor is there a provision, in the case of a recalcitrant claimant or a reluctant respondent guilty of a similar act, that requires the arbitrator to either proceed on an *ex parte* basis or to dismiss a claim for want of prosecution. In such cases, it is entirely the arbitrator's decision to act upon this, if absolutely satisfied that to do so follows the highest principles of natural justice. The act, at article 25, regarding default of a party, as well as the rules based on the UNCITRAL Model Law, do give the arbitrator such powers to act in the case of "want or lack of prosecution" – in the sense that they may "subject to the provisions of the law, conduct the arbitration in such a manner as is considered appropriate". The Arbitration Act, 2017, Part 5, Conduct of Arbitral Proceedings, explains this in greater detail.

42. **Costs**: This matter was briefly referred to earlier. An important aspect of the award is costs – that is, who the arbitrator decides must bear the costs of the proceedings and who pays for the various costs of the arbitration. Generally, the arbitrator has no choice but to conform to the relative law on the subject. Guidance on this subject was given prior to the Jamaican Arbitration Act, 2017 by the old legislation: "The costs of the reference and the award shall be in the discretion of the arbitrator or umpire who may direct to and by whom and in what manner those costs or any part thereof shall be paid, and may tax or settle the amount of costs to be so paid or any part thereof and may award costs to be paid as between solicitor and client."

We are further guided on the definition and the limitation of costs by the UNICITAL Rules, article 38:

   (a) The fees of the arbitral tribunal to be stated separately as to each arbitrator.

   (b) The travel and other expenses incurred by the arbitrators.

   (c) The costs of expert advice and of other assistance required by the arbitral tribunal.

   (d) The travel and other expenses to the extent such expenses are approved by the tribunal.

   (e) The costs for legal representation and assistance of the successful party if such costs were claimed during the arbitral proceedings, and only to the extent that the arbitral tribunal determines that the amount of such costs is reasonable.

   (f) Any fees and expenses of the appointing authority.

Not included in the above are costs I usually allow in awards are the reasonable costs in connection with hiring suitable accommodation for the hearing and reasonable expenses and incidentals connected thereto.

How does an arbitrator apportion costs? The usual method is to state in the award that the losing party is to pay the winning party their own and the other side's costs incurred in the case. The rule is that *costs follow the event.* There are few exceptions to that rigid rule, unless there is credible evidence that the winner has done something calculated to unnecessarily delay or obfuscate, or has done something wrong during the course of the arbitration or has acted unreasonably or oppressively. In such instances – or others, at the arbitrator's discretion – the award of costs can be adjusted commensurately.

Similarly, occasions may arise where one party is only partially successful, in which case the decision of apportionment of responsibility of costs lies with the arbitrator. In instances where the parties are unable to agree upon the extent and value of costs in regard to claims and counterclaims, the final decision may be left to the arbitrator to adjudicate. Where this is not possible, or where the arbitrator abstains, the issue may be referred to the court for settlement.

There are many more complications inherent in the subject of costs, especially in large, important or international cases; such matters are contained in great detail in the many books on this subject.

Index

www.ingramcontent.com/pod-product-compliance
Lightning Source LLC
Chambersburg PA
CBHW021602210326
41599CB00010B/555